Thanks for your Purchase! Scan the Code for FREE Books!

Please, be so kind to scan the other code below to Review the Book!

The recipes and information in this book are provided for educational purposes only. Everyone needs are different, and these recipes and methods reflect specifically on what has worked for the author. This book is not intended to provide medical advice or take the place of medical treatment from qualified health care professionals. All readers who are taking any form of prescription medication should consult with their physicians before making any changes to their current eating habits. Neither the publisher nor the author takes any responsibility for any possible consequences of any person reading or following the information in this book.

TABLE OF CONTENTS

Dr Sebi Cookbook	4

VEGETABLES & FRUIT 5
- Roasted Okra 6
- Wild Rice Stuffed Peppers 7
- Stir-Fried Watercress with Ginger 8
- Sesame Turnip Greens 9
- Zucchini Fritters 10
- Roasted Sweet Potato and Spinach Bowl 11
- Alkaline Zucchini Coleslaw 12
- Kale Pesto with Roasted Butternut Squash 13
- The Greatest Greens 14
- Stuffed Bell Pepper 15
- Vegetable Mushroom Sauce 16
- Home-Style Okra 17
- Fruit Skewers 18
- Amaranth Date-Walnut Breakfast 19
- Vegan Apple Turnovers 20

SOUPS & SUCES 21
- Habanero Mango Salsa 22
- Butternut Soup 23
- Classic Hummus 24
- Spicy Soup 25
- Bone Broth 26
- Herbed Mushroom Stew 27
- Alkaline Electric Apple Sauce 28

SALADS 29
- Stuffed Avocado Salad 30
- Ultimate Lettuce Cups 31
- Cucumber Dill Salad 32
- Apple Walnut Arugula Salad 33
- Spelt grain salad with ginger tahini dressing 34
- Curry Broccoli Salad 35

BREAKFASTS & DESSERTS 36
- Strawberry Ice Cream 37
- Fruity Yogurt 38
- Green Detox Smoothie 39
- Electric Banana cream pie 40
- Strawberry Banana ice-cream 41
- Veggie Omelette 42
- Papaya Breakfast Shake 43

TABLE OF CONTENTS

LEGUMES	**44**
Garbanzo Burger	45
Alkaline Potato Salad styled Garbanzo	46
Electric Meatballs	47
Chickpea and Mushroom soup with Zucchini noodles	48
Chickpea Burger	49

PASTA & GRAINS	**50**
Creamy Veggie Pasta	51
Electric Macaroni and Cheese	52
Electric Walnut pesto Pasta	53
Alkaline Creamy Kamut Pasta	54
Mexican-Style Quinoa	55
Sushi Roll	56
Mediterranean Kamut	57
Breakfast Skillet	58
Cherry Berry Bars	59
Alkaline Blackberry Breakfast bars	60

PANCAKES & WRAPS	**61**
Savory Jumbo Pancakes	62
Banana Pancakes	63
Blueberries Muffins	64
Alkaline Electric Tacos	65
Alkaline Veggie Fajitas	66
Alkaline Electric Flatbread	67
Alkaline Blueberry Spelt Pancakes	68
Squash falafels	69
Spelt Strawberry Waffles	70
Vegetable Patties	71

The Schedules	**72**

Dr Sebi Alkaline Diet Cookbook

Thank you first for getting this cookbook. Here you will be provided all the tools to take a healthy Dr Sebi-Based Alkaline Diet. Prepare recipes that are quick and easy to prepare and budget friendly. I sincerely hope that you will enjoy the recipes and guidance offered in this cookbook.

As a Thank you, I would like you to join on Facebook my FREE Books Page, where you will be messaged free books, both kindle and paperback when available.

Click on the link below and start enjoying them from today!

https://bit.ly/BooksGaloreDeal

VEGETABLES & FRUIT

ROASTED OKRA	6
WILD RICE STUFFED PEPPERS	7
STIR-FRIED WATERCRESS WITH GINGER	8
SESAME TURNIP GREENS	9
ZUCCHINI FRITTERS	10
ROASTED SWEET POTATO AND SPINACH BOWL	11
ALKALINE ZUCCHINI COLESLAW	12
KALE PESTO WITH ROASTED BUTTERNUT SQUASH	13
THE GREATEST GREENS	14
STUFFED BELL PEPPER	15
VEGETABLE MUSHROOM SAUCE	16
HOME-STYLE OKRA	17
FRUIT SKEWERS	18
AMARANTH DATE-WALNUT BREAKFAST	19
VEGAN APPLE TURNOVERS	20

Roasted Okra

NUTRITIONAL VALUES

Amount per Servings, 200 Calories | 14.48 g Fat | 17.14 g Total Carbs | 7.4 g Fiber | 4.43 g Protein

Prep Time	10 min
Cooking Time	25 min
Total Time	35 min
Servings	2

INGREDIENTS

1 lb. okra

2 Tbsp avocado oil

1 Tsp thyme

1/4 Tsp cayenne pepper

1/4 Tsp sea salt

DIRECTIONS

1. Preheat the oven to 400F and line a baking sheet with parchment paper.
2. Thoroughly wash the okra and pat dry the excess moisture.
3. Trim the okra by cutting off the stem ends and the tips. Now cut the okra in half lengthwise.
4. Place the okra in a large bowl. Add thyme, cayenne pepper and salt.
5. Drizzle oil and stir to coat evenly.
6. Now place the okra onto the prepared baking sheet in a single layer and bake in preheated oven for 25 minutes, flipping twice during the roasting time until golden brown.
7. Serve and Enjoy!

Wild Rice Stuffed

NUTRITIONAL VALUES

Amount per Servings, 326 Calories | 8.51 g Fat | 55.9 g Total Carbs | 6.3 g Fiber | 11.28 g Protein

Prep Time	15 min
Cooking Time	35 min
Total Time	50 min
Servings	6

INGREDIENTS

- bell peppers, tops removed and seeded
- 2 cups wild rice, cooked
- 1/3 cup toasted walnuts, chopped
- 1 cup tomatoes, chopped
- 1 cup mushrooms, sliced
- 1 medium zucchini, diced
- 1/2 cup onion, finely chopped
- 2 **Tbsp** grapeseed oil, divided
- 1 **Tsp** onion powder
- 1 **Tsp** thyme
- Sea salt, to taste
- 1 yellow squash, diced

DIRECTIONS

1. Heat oven to 400F and grease a baking dish with some oil.
2. Using a sharp knife, slice off the top of the bell pepper, reserving the tops.
3. Place the pepper flat end on a cutting board and separate the white inner core, set aside.
4. Heat oil in a large skillet over medium-high heat.
5. Add onion and sauté until slightly golden brown.
6. Add tomatoes, mushrooms, zucchini, squash, onion powder, thyme and salt; cook for about 10 minutes until vegetables are tender.
7. Stir in rice and cook for 5 minutes more.
8. Place the prepared bell peppers into the baking dish.
9. Stuff each pepper with the rice mixture.
10. Place the reserved tops on each stuffed pepper.
11. Drizzle 1 tablespoon of oil on all over the peppers.
12. Cover the dish with aluminum foil and bake for 10 minutes.
13. Remove the foil and bake for 5 minutes more until topping is slightly crisp.
14. Garnish with chopped toasted walnuts and serve.

Stir-Fried Watercress with Ginger

NUTRITIONAL VALUES

Amount per Servings, 61 Calories | 4.72 g Fat | 2.92 g Total Carbs | 1 g Fiber | 3.66 g Protein

Prep Time	10 min
Cooking Time	30 min
Total Time	40 min
Servings	6

INGREDIENTS

- 2lbs. fresh watercress
- 1/2 cup tomato, chopped
- 1 knob fresh ginger, minced
- 1/4 cup spring water
- 1 **Tsp** onion powder
- 2 **Tbsp** grapeseed oil
- Sea salt, to taste

DIRECTIONS

1. Discard any slightly yellow and limp sprigs from the watercress.
2. Using a sharp knife, trim the thick stalks from the watercress.
3. Thoroughly wash the cress and spin it dry. Pat dry with paper towels if still wet to remove all moisture.
4. Heat the oil in a wok or large-skillet over medium heat.
5. Add ginger and tomatoes, sauté for 5 minutes.
6. Pour in the water, reduce the heat to low and cook until peels begin to detach from the tomato flesh. Stir well to form a paste.
7. Add watercress, onion powder and salt to the tomato paste, cook for 15 minutes, turning occasionally with tongs until tender.
8. Taste and adjust the salt if needed.

Sesame Turnip Greens

NUTRITIONAL VALUES

Amount per Servings, 152 Calories | 5.65 g Fat | 24.48 g Total Carbs | 10.6 g Fiber | 5.6 g Protein

Prep Time	10 min
Cooking Time	40 min
Total Time	50 min
Servings	6

INGREDIENTS

- 4 lbs. turnip greens
- 1 cup onion, finely chopped
- 2 cups spring water
- 1 **Tbsp** sesame oil
- 3 **Tbsp** sesame seeds
- Sea salt, to taste
- 1 **Tsp** date sugar
- 1 **Tsp** black pepper

DIRECTIONS

1. Cut off and discard the discolored leaves from the greens.
2. Wash the greens thoroughly in a colander.
3. Now stack several leaves and slice them crosswise into 1-inch thick pieces.
4. Heat sesame oil to a skillet, over medium heat.
5. Add onion and sauté until slightly brown.
6. Add in turnip greens and season with some salt and black pepper.
7. Pour in the water and bring greens to a boil.
8. Reduce the heat to low and let simmer for 35 minutes.
9. Once the water is cooked off, add date sugar and mix well.
10. Sprinkle sesame seeds on top and serve.

Zucchini Fritters

NUTRITIONAL VALUES

Amount per Servings, 69 Calories | 4.89 g Fat | 5.3 g Total Carbs | 1.3 g Fiber | 1.46 g Protein

Prep Time	10 min
Cooking Time	15 min
Total Time	25 min
Servings	6

INGREDIENTS

- 2 large zucchini
- 1 large bell pepper, chopped
- 1/2 cup onion, chopped
- 1/4 cup spring water
- 1/4 cup chickpea flour
- 1 **Tsp** onion powder
- 1 **Tbsp** dill
- 1 **Tsp** thyme
- Sea salt, to taste
- 2 **Tbsp** sesame oil

DIRECTIONS

1. Peel and thoroughly wash the zucchini and pat the excess moisture with a paper-towel.
2. Using a sharp knife cut off the ends, slice into halves and scoop out the seeds to discard.
3. Now simply shred the zucchini pieces using a food processor or a hand grater.
4. Place the shredded zucchini in a colander and set over a bowl.
5. Sprinkle some salt, mix well and allow to stand for 10 minutes.
6. Meanwhile add chopped bell pepper, onion and chickpea flour to a bowl.
7. Add in onion powder, dill, thyme and salt.
8. Slowly add in water, stir to combine until forms a thick lumpy batter.
9. Let the batter rest for 10 minutes to get even thicker.
10. Next using your clean hands or a cheese cloth, squeeze out as much liquid from the zucchini as possible.
11. Transfer the squeezed zucchini into the prepared batter, gently fold to combine.
12. Add oil to a large pan over medium-high heat.
13. Once hot, scoop two tablespoon mound of batter into the hot oil, pressing slightly with a spatula.
14. Cook until both sides are nice golden brown, about 2 minutes each side.
15. Add 2-3 fritters at a time, spacing them at least 2 inches apart.
16. Repeat with the rest of the batter.
17. Once the fritters are done, transfer to a paper towel-lined plate and serve warm.

Roasted Sweet Potato and Spinach Bowl

NUTRITIONAL VALUES

Amount per Servings, 254 Calories | 12 g Fat | 34.3 g Total Carbs | 5.5 g Fiber | 4.6 g Protein

Prep Time	10 min
Cooking Time	30 min
Total Time	40 min
Servings	4 min

INGREDIENTS

- 3 cups sweet potatoes (Peeled and diced)
- 2 tsp garlic (Minced)
- 2 cups spinach
- 1 tsp sea salt
- 2 tsp sesame seeds
- 2 tbsp olive oil
- 4 tbsp pumpkin seeds

DIRECTIONS

1. Pre-heat the oven at 350 degrees Fahrenheit.
2. In a baking tray, toss sweet potatoes with 1 tbsp olive oil and sea salt.
3. Bake the potatoes for 20 to 25 minutes or until fork-tender.
4. In a pan, heat 1 tbsp grapeseed oil to medium heat.
5. Add spinach to the pan and sauté for 3 to 4 minutes. Set it aside.
6. In 4 bowls, equally, divide roasted potatoes and spinach.
7. Top each bowl with 1 tbsp of pumpkin seed and ½ tsp of sesame seeds and serve.

Alkaline Zucchini Coleslaw

NUTRITIONAL VALUES

Amount per Servings, 50 Calories | 0.3 g Fat | 7 g Total Carbs | 1.4 g Fiber | 2.1 g Protein

Prep Time	15 min
Cooking Time	0 min
Total Time	0 min
Servings	4 min

INGREDIENTS

- 2 cups Zucchini (Shredded)
- ½ cup Butternut squash (Shredded)
- ¼ cup Red onion (Diced)
- ½ cup Brazil Nuts
- ¼ cup Hemp Milk
- ½ tsp Lime Juice
- 1 tsp Sea Moss
- ½ Sea salt
- ½ cup Spring water
- 1 tbsp Dates

DIRECTIONS

1. Soak the brazil nuts in water overnight.
2. In a food processor or blender, add drained brazil nuts, dates, hemp milk, sea moss, sea salt, and ¼ cup of spring water. Blend it for a minute or two.
3. Gradually add remaining ¼ cup of spring water in the mixture and blend to adjust the consistency.
4. In a bowl, toss shredded zucchini, butternut squash, and onion. Gradually add brazil nut mixture and mix.
5. Refrigerate the mixture for 1 to 2 hours.
6. Serve chilled.

Kale Pesto with Roasted Butternut Squash

NUTRITIONAL VALUES

Amount per Servings, 1127 Calories | 41.2 g Fat | 160.5 g Total Carbs | 19.1 g Fiber | 34 g Protein

Prep Time	40 min
Cooking Time	30 min
Total Time	40 min
Servings	4 min

INGREDIENTS

- 3 cups butternut squash (Cubed)
- 2 tbsp grapeseed oil
- 1 tbsp dried sage
- 1 tbsp dried thyme
- 1 tsp sea salt
- 4 cups kale (Without stems)
- 5 tbsp fresh parsley
- 6-7 tbsp lime juice
- ¾ cup brazil nuts
- 2 tbsp onion powder
- 5 cups cooked quinoa (To serve)
- 1/2 cup watercress (Garnish, optional)
- ½ cup cherry tomatoes (Garnish, optional)

DIRECTIONS

1. Preheat the oven at 400 F.
2. In a baking tray, toss cubed squash, grapeseed oil, dried sage, dried thyme and sea salt. Bake the seasoned squash for 30 minutes until golden and seas fork tender. Cool them at room temperature.
3. In a food processor, add kale, fresh parsley, lime juice, olive oil, brazil nuts and onion powder. Blend them into a pesto consistency.
4. In a bowl, toss kale pesto and squash together and garnish with watercress and cherry tomatoes.
5. Serve with cooked quinoa.

The Greatest Greens

NUTRITIONAL VALUES

Amount per Servings Calories: 98kcal| Protein: 1.5 g | Carbohydrates 18 g| fat: 1 g |

Prep Time	15 min
Cook Time	20 min
Total Time	20 min
Servings	6 min

INGREDIENTS

- 3 bunches of mustard and turnips greens
- 2 cups chopped onions
- 1/4 cup olive oil
- 1 tsp of cayenne or chili powder
- 3 tbsp sea salt

DIRECTIONS

1. Heat pan then add onions, cook till golden brown.
2. Add greens, cook down for 20 min.
3. Season with sea salt, and cayenne or chili powder and serve.

Stuffed Bell Pepper

NUTRITIONAL VALUES

Amount per Servings Calories 408kcal | protein: 32g |Carbohydrate: 25 g | fat: 20g |

Prep Time	20 min
Cook Time	60 min
Total Time	80 min
Servings	6 min

INGREDIENTS

- peppers chopped fine
- 1/4 tsp of ground cumin
- 6 slices of kamut or spelt bread toasted, crumbled
- Quinoa grains
- 1 1/2 cup of quinoa
- 1/2 tsp sweet basil
- 1/2 tsp sea salt
- 1 lb. oyster or brown button mushroom
- 2 green bell peppers

DIRECTIONS

1. Steam bell peppers until tender, then hollow out.
2. Place quinoa grain in a saucepan with water covering the top.
3. Cook low heat until water is absorbed, and then set aside.
4. Sauté mushrooms and red bell peppers in olive oil.
5. Season in bell peppers with some spices and olive oil.
6. Mix quinoa, mushrooms, and red bell pepper with remaining seasonings.
7. Stuff bell peppers with mixture, then sprinkle breadcrumbs on top.
8. Bake in preheated oven at 400F for 10-15 minutes.
9. Serve hot and enjoy with a green leafy salad.

Vegetable Mushroom Soup

NUTRITIONAL VALUES

Amount per Servings Calories: 205kcal | protein: 5.4 g | |carbohydrates: 12.5 g | fat: 16.6 g|

Prep Time	10 min
Cook Time	30 min
Total Time	40 min
Servings	4 min

INGREDIENTS

- 1 lb oyster mushrooms, chopped
- 1 cup quinoa
- 1/2 lb kamut spiral pasta Spring water
- 1 large chayote squash, peeled and chopped
- 2-3 bunches kale
- 1 tsp Oregano
- 1 tsp Cumin
- 1 small red and green bell pepper chopped
- 1 bunch spinach, washed, and steamed
- 1 tbs olive oil
- 1 onion chopped finely
- 1 tsp Thyme
- 1 tsp Marjoram

DIRECTIONS

1. Put olive oil in a hot skillet.
2. Sauté mushrooms, bell peppers, and onions slowly for 20 minutes.
3. Add mushroom mixture in soup pot and fill with spring water.
4. Add chayote squash.
5. Add thyme, marjoram, rosemary, oregano, red pepper, cumin, clove, and quinoa.
6. Simmer for 45 minutes.
7. Add Kamut Pasta and simmer for 15 min.
8. Add spinach, stir, and then serve when tender.

Home-Style Okra

NUTRITIONAL VALUES

Amount per Servings Calories: 182kcal | Protein: 2 g | |Carbohydrate: 12 g |Total Fat: 14g |

Prep Time	20 min
Cook Time	25 min
Total Time	45 min
Servings	3 min

INGREDIENTS

- 4 tbs olive oil
- 1/4 tsp African red pepper 1/4 tsp. sassafras
- 1/4 tsp. sea salt
- cooked wild rice or quinoa
- Fresh okra diced
- 2 soft tomatoes
- 1/2 yellow onion chopped fine
- 1/4 tsp ground cumin

DIRECTIONS

1. Heat oil in a pan. Add cumin seeds and let it splutter.
2. Next, add green chili and chopped onion. Cook for 2 minutes on a low flame.
3. Add turmeric powder, mix well.
4. Next, add the okra and cook for 5-6 minutes on a medium flame. Stir when required.
5. Finally, add salt, coriander powder and dry mango powder.
6. Mix well. Cover and cook till done. Stir when required.
7. Switch off the flame. Add coriander powder and lime juice. Mix well.
8. Serve hot with roti or paratha. This also tastes good with dal and rice.

Fruit Skewers

NUTRITIONAL VALUES

Amount per Servings, 298 Calories | 0.76 g Fat | 79.1 g Total Carbs | 5.1 g Fiber | 1.75 g Protein

Prep Time	15 min
Cooking Time	5 min
Total Time	20 min
Servings	4

INGREDIENTS

- 1 cup watermelon, seeded and cubed
- 2 medium apples, cubed
- 3 peaches, cubed
- 1 cup mangoes, cubed
- 5-6 plums, halved
- 1/2 cup agave syrup
- 2 tablespoon lime juice

DIRECTIONS

1. Toss apples, peaches, mangoes, plum and lime juice in a bowl.

2. Now alternately thread each skewer with watermelon, apple, peaches, mangoes and plums.

3. Drizzle agave syrup and serve immediately.

Amaranth Date-Walnut Breakfast

NUTRITIONAL VALUES

Amount per Servings, 504 Calories | 22.81 g Fat | 69.34 g Total Carbs | 6.2 g Fiber | 11.71 g Protein

Prep Time	10 min
Cooking Time	25 min
Total Time	35 min
Servings	6

INGREDIENTS

- 2 cups amaranth
- 4 cups spring water
- 1 cup walnuts, chopped
- 1/2 cup dates, pitted and chopped
- 1 cup coconut milk
- 1/2 cup agave syrup
- 1/4 tsp salt

DIRECTIONS

1. In a medium-sized saucepan over medium-low heat, add amaranth and water.
2. Cover and bring to a boil, once the amaranth starts to bubble reduce the heat to low and let it simmer for 25 minutes, stirring occasionally until liquid is cooked off.
3. Once finished cooking remove from the heat, allowing to stand for 10 minutes.
4. Stir in salt and mix well.
5. Divide the amaranth among serving bowls.
6. Add walnuts and dates.

Vegan Apple Turnovers

NUTRITIONAL VALUES

Amount per Servings, 450 Calories | 18.9 g Fat | 55 g Total Carbs | 7.2 g Fiber | 0.8 g Protein

Prep Time	40 min
Cooking Time	49 min
Total Time	80 min
Servings	4 mint

INGREDIENTS

- 5-6 apples (peeled and diced)
- 2 cups white spelt flour
- 5 tbsp coconut palm sugar
- 1/3 cup grapeseed oil
- ¾ cup spring water
- ½ tsp sea salt
- 2 tsp allspice
- 3 tbsp lime juice
- 1 tsp ground clove
- 2 tbsp agave

DIRECTIONS

1. Toss the diced apples in the lime juice to avoid browning.
2. In a bowl, mix white spelt flour, 3 tbsp coconut palm sugar, and ¼ tsp sea salt.
3. Gradually add grapeseed oil in the flour mixture and mix.
4. Gradually add spring water and knead the mixture until it forms a dough.
5. Knead the dough for a minute and place it in a greased bowl. Cover the bowl and chill it for 30 minutes.
6. In a pan, heat 1 tbsp of grapeseed oil to medium heat.
7. Add diced apples, 2 tbsp coconut palm sugar, ¼ tsp sea salt, ground clove, agave, and allspice.
8. Cook for 10 minutes or until apples is soft.
9. Transfer apples into a bowl, cover, and chill them for 20 minutes.
10. Preheat the oven at 350 Fahrenheit.
11. Transfer the dough on the floured surface and knead for 2 to 3 minutes.
12. Divide the dough into 8 equal parts.
13. Roll out each dough balls into circles.
14. Place 1 ½ tbsp of the apple mixture in the center and turn over the dough over the apples by pushing out air.
15. With a fork seal the corners of the turnover. Repeat with all dough balls.
16. Line a baking tray with a parchment paper. Place the turnovers on the tray.
17. Bake them for 10 to 12 minutes.
18. Cool them and serve.

SOUPS & SAUCES

Habanero Mango Salsa	22
Butternut Soup	23
Classic Hummus	24
Spicy Soup	25
Bone Broth	26
Herbed Mushroom Stew	27
Alkaline Electric Apple Sauce	28

Habanero Mango Salsa

NUTRITIONAL VALUES

Amount per Servings, 155 Calories | 7.86 g Fat | 21.9 g Total Carbs | 6.8 g Fiber | 3.05 g Protein

Prep Time	10 min
Cooking Time	15 min
Total Time	15 min
Servings	4

INGREDIENTS

- 2 large Roma tomatoes, diced
- 1 large mango, pitted and finely diced
- 1 avocado, diced
- 1 large onion, chopped
- 1 habanero pepper, minced
- 1 **Tbsp** date sugar
- 1 **Tsp** sea salt
- 2 **Tbsp** lime juice

DIRECTIONS

1. Put the diced tomatoes, mango, avocado, onion and pepper in a medium bowl.

2. Using a large spoon, stir the ingredients together.

3. Add in lime juice, sugar and salt, toss until well combined.

4. Taste and adjust salt, if needed.

5. Let the salsa rest for 10 minutes or longer in refrigerator.

Butternut Soup

NUTRITIONAL VALUES

Amount per Servings, 93 Calories | 5.29 g Fat | 12.27 g Total Carbs | 3.5 g Fiber | 1.25 g Protein

Prep Time	15 min
Cooking Time	4-7 hrs
Total Time	7hr- 15 min
Servings	6

INGREDIENTS

- 1 medium butternut squash, seeded, peeled and cut into cubes
- 4 cups vegetable broth
- 1 medium apple, cored and roughly chopped
- 1 medium onion, roughly chopped
- 1 sprig sage
- 1 Tbsp fresh thyme, minced
- 1/4 Tsp cayenne pepper
- 2 Tbsp olive oil
- Sea salt and freshly ground black pepper to taste
- 2 Tbsp fresh rosemary, minced

DIRECTIONS

1. Add butternut squash, apple, onion and herbs into a slow cooker.
2. Season with some salt and pepper, toss to combine.
3. Pour in the broth, cover and cook for 6-7 hours on low, or 3-4 hours on high.
4. Once the squash is completely tender, remove and discard the sage.
5. Puree the soup using an immersion blender.
6. Taste and season with additional salt, pepper and cayenne as needed.
7. Transfer the soup into bowl, drizzle olive oil on top and serve.

Classic Hummus

NUTRITIONAL VALUES

Amount per Servings, 325 Calories | 21.62 g Fat | 26.13 g Total Carbs | 6.9 g Fiber | 9.34 g Protein

Prep Time	5 min
Cooking Time	5 min
Total Time	10 min
Servings	4

INGREDIENTS

- 1 cup Garbanzo Bean Flour
- 1/2 cup Onions, diced
- 1 Plum Tomato, diced
- 2 tsp. Basil
- 1 tsp. Dill
- 1/2 tsp. Ginger Powder
- 2 cups garbanzo Beans Half Cooked
- 1/4 Tsp cayenne pepper
- 1/2 Tsp sea salt
- 1/2 cup Green Peppers, diced

DIRECTIONS

1. Add beans, tahini, lime juice, 3 tablespoon oil, water, onion powder, ginger powder and salt to a high-powered blender.

2. Blend the beans on high speed for 30 seconds, pause once or twice to scrape the sides down.

3. If the hummus seems too thick, add a tablespoon of water.

4. Transfer the hummus into a large bowl.

5. Using the back of a large spoon create swirls in the center.

6. Drizzle remaining tablespoon of oil and sprinkle cayenne pepper.

Spicy Soup

NUTRITIONAL VALUES

Amount per Servings, 97 Calories | 7.47 g Fat | 7.15 g Total Carbs | 2.3 g Fiber | 2.45 g Protein

Prep Time	10 min
Cooking Time	45 min
Total Time	55 min
Servings	4

INGREDIENTS

- 6 cups spring water
- 2-1/2 cup tomatoes, chopped
- 2 large zucchini, sliced
- 1 large bell pepper, cubed
- 2 cups mushrooms, sliced
- 1 cup kale
- 1/2 cup onion, chopped
- 2 Tbsp avocado oil
- 1 bay leaf, crumbled
- 1 Tsp thyme
- 1 Tsp cayenne pepper
- 1/2 Tsp sage
- Sea salt, to taste

DIRECTIONS

1. Heat a large pot over medium-high heat.
2. Add oil and heat until shimmering.
3. Add onion and sauté until translucent, about 5 minutes.
4. Immediately add in the tomatoes, 1/2 cup of water, bay leaf, thyme, cayenne pepper, sage and salt.
5. Cover and let simmer on low until tomatoes are softened and forms into a thick sauce mixture.
6. Add in zucchini, bell pepper, mushrooms and kale, cook for 5 minutes.
7. Add water, cover and let cook on low for 35 minutes until veggies are cooked through.
8. Remove from the heat and ladle the soup into bowls

Bone Broth

NUTRITIONAL VALUES

Amount per Servings, 47 Calories | 0.5 g Fat | 9.96 g Total Carbs | 2.8 g Fiber | 2.83 g Protein

Prep Time	15 min
Cooking Time	4-8 hrs
Total Time	8hr-15min
Servings	4

INGREDIENTS

- 12 cups spring water
- 1 cup dandelion greens, chopped
- 2 cups mushrooms, sliced
- 2 cups kale, chopped
- 1 cup plum tomatoes, chopped
- 1 large onion, cubed
- 1 Tbsp ginger, grated
- 1 Tbsp powdered seaweed
- 1 bay leaf
- 3-4 cloves
- Sea salt, to taste

DIRECTIONS

3. Rinse the vegetables thoroughly under cold running water.
4. Add all the veggies and water into the bottom of the slow cooker. If you don't have a slow cooker, you can use a Dutch oven.
5. Add in seaweed, bay leaf, cloves and salt, give a good stir.
6. Cover and cook on LOW for 8 hours or HIGH for 4 hours.
7. Once done cooking, let cool at room temperature for about 10 minutes.
8. Strain the broth into a bowl, using a fine mesh sieve and discard the solids.
9. Store the broth in an air-tight container.
1. Store in refrigerator for up to 5-7 days.
2. Drink it on its own or use it to make soups, pasta, quinoa or whatever recipe calls for the broth.

Herbed Mushroom Stew

NUTRITIONAL VALUES

Amount per Servings, 154 Calories | 12.84 g Fat | 8.54 g Total Carbs | 2.6 g Fiber | 4.17 g Protein

Prep Time	10 min
Cooking Time	45 min
Total Time	55 min
Servings	4

INGREDIENTS

- 1lb. baby bella mushrooms
- 1-1/2 cup vegetable broth (Dr. Sebi approved)
- 1/2 cup olives
- 1/4 cup onion, chopped
- 2 cups cherry tomatoes, halved
- 3 Tbsp avocado oil
- 1 Tbsp oregano
- 1 tbs olive oil 1/2 red bell
- 1 Tsp dried basil
- 1 Tsp thyme
- 1 Tsp sage
- Dash of cayenne pepper
- Sea salt, to taste

DIRECTIONS

1. Rinse the mushrooms thoroughly to remove any dirt and then pat dry.
2. Slice the mushrooms and olives; set aside.
3. Heat a large skillet over a medium heat. Add oil and chopped onion; cook until they begin to brown, about 5 minutes.
4. Add mushrooms and cook until they let off moisture and are golden brown.
5. Immediately add in the tomatoes, herbs and salt.
6. Pour broth and stir well to ensure that the flavors are dispersed evenly.
7. Reduce the heat to low and cook for 20 minutes.
8. Once the stew has simmered, add in the olives and cook for 10 minutes more.
9. Remove from the heat and serve warm.

Alkaline Electric Apple Sauce

NUTRITIONAL VALUES

Amount per Servings, Calories: 142kcal | Protein: 1g| |Carbohydrates:38g|Fat 1g|

Prep Time	20 min
Cook Time	0 min
Total Time	20 min
Servings	5 min

INGREDIENTS

3 cups apples peeled and chopped
3 tbsp agave
1 Tsp lime juice
spring water (optional)
strawberries* (optional)
1 Tsp sea moss gel (optional)
1 tsp Salt
Cloves

DIRECTIONS

1. Put chopped apples together with salt, cloves, lime juice and agave in the blender.

2. Pulse with the mixer to achieve the desired consistency.

3. Stir in strawberries until everything is well mixed.

4. Add 1 tablespoon of spring water in case it does not mix well.

5. Serve and enjoy! Keep leftovers in the fridge.

SALADS

Stuffed Avocado Salad	**30**
Ultimate Lettuce Cups	**31**
Cucumber Dill Salad	**32**
Apple Walnut Arugula Salad	**33**
Spelt grain salad with ginger tahini dressing	**34**
Curry Broccoli Salad	**35**

Stuffed Avocado Salad

NUTRITIONAL VALUES

Amount per Servings, 230 Calories | 15.64 g Fat | 21.44 g Total Carbs | 9.8 g Fiber | 5.31 g Protein

Prep Time	15 min
Cooking Time	5 min
Total Time	20 min
Servings	4

INGREDIENTS

- 2 large avocados
- 1-1/2 cup chickpeas, cooked
- 1 Roma tomato, chopped
- 1 small onion, chopped
- 1 teaspoon dill
- 2 Tsp fresh tarragon, minced
- 1 Tsp sweet basil
- 1 Tsp agave syrup
- Sea salt, to taste

DIRECTIONS

1. Combine chickpeas, tomatoes, onion, dill, tarragon, basil and salt to a bowl.

2. Slice the avocados in half and remove the pit.

3. Using a sharp knife make cubes and then carefully remove with the spoon. Be careful not to break through the peel.

4. Add cubes to the chickpea mixture, stir well to combine.

5. Spoon the salad back into the avocado cups.

6. Drizzle agave syrup and sprinkle some more salt on top, serve immediately and enjoy!

Ultimate Lettuce Cups

NUTRITIONAL VALUES

Amount per Servings, 105 Calories | 7.55 g Fat | 8.74 g Total Carbs | 4.6 g Fiber | 2.93 g Protein

Prep Time	15 min
Cooking Time	20 min
Total Time	35 min
Servings	6

INGREDIENTS

- 1 medium-sized romaine lettuce head
- 1 medium zucchini
- 1 cup cherry tomatoes, halved
- 1 cup olives, sliced
- 1/2 cup onion, sliced
- 1/4 cup raisins
- 1 Tbsp avocado oil
- 1 Tbsp lime juice
- 2 Tsp hemp seeds hulled
- 1 Tsp oregano
- Sea salt, to taste

DIRECTIONS

1. Preheat oven to 425F. Line a baking sheet with aluminum foil or parchment paper and lightly grease with oil. Set aside.
2. Trim the zucchini ends and then slice into half.
3. Next cut the halves into 1/2-inch sticks.
4. Season with some salt and place onto the prepared baking sheet.
5. Drizzle oil and mix well.
6. Bake for 15-20 minutes, flipping halfway through until golden and crispy.
7. While the zucchini is baking, combine cherry tomatoes, olives, onion, raisins and hemp seeds to a bowl.
8. Stir in lime juice, oregano and some salt.
9. Lay out the romaine lettuce leaves; add a spoonful of prepared filling.
10. Top with crispy zucchini and serve immediately.

Cucumber Dill Salad

NUTRITIONAL VALUES

Amount per Servings, 135 Calories | 12.46 g Fat | 6.66 g Total Carbs | 3.1 g Fiber | 1.54 g Protein

Prep Time	15 min
Cooking Time	25 min
Total Time	40 min
Servings	4

INGREDIENTS

- 2 medium cucumbers, thinly sliced
- 2 cups arugula
- 1 large avocado, diced
- 1/4 cup black currants
- 2 **Tbsp** dill, chopped
- 2 **Tbsp** lime juice
- 2 **Tbsp** olive oil
- 1/4 **Tsp** cayenne pepper
- Sea salt and black pepper, to taste

DIRECTIONS

1. In a mason jar or a small bowl, whisk together the lime juice and olive oil, until blended. Season with salt and pepper.

2. Add sliced cucumber, arugula, avocados, currants and dill to a bowl.

3. Pour the dressing on top and toss well to coat evenly.

4. Sprinkle cayenne pepper on top.

5. Refrigerate until chilled about 20 minutes.

6. Serve and enjoy!

Apple Walnut Arugula Salad

NUTRITIONAL VALUES

Amount per Servings, 285 Calories | 23.34 g Fat | 19.26 g Total Carbs | 5.2 g Fiber | 5.03 g Protein

Prep Time	15 min
Cooking Time	10 min
Total Time	25 min
Servings	4

INGREDIENTS

- 4 cups young arugula leaves
- 1 cup walnuts
- 2 small apples
- 1 cup cherry tomatoes
- 1 large cucumber
- 1/2 cup olives, sliced
- 1 habanero pepper, seeds removed

For Dressing:
- 3 **Tbsp** lime juice
- 2 **Tbsp** olive oil
- 1 **Tsp** thyme
- Sea salt, to taste

DIRECTIONS

1. Start by preparing a dressing; combine all the dressing ingredients to a mixing bowl.
2. Whisk vigorously to combine. Taste and adjust flavor as needed.
3. Preheat the oven to 400F and line a baking sheet with parchment paper.
4. Spread out the walnuts evenly onto the prepared baking sheet.
5. Toast for 10 minutes until browned and fragrant, stirring occasionally.
6. While the walnuts are toasting, thoroughly wash the arugula leaves, tomatoes and cucumber.
7. Now chop the cucumber into cubes and mince the pepper.
8. Using a vegetable peeler, remove the peel from the apple flesh.
9. Cut the apple in half and turn the halves flat side down and cut them in half again to yield quarters.
10. Remove the core and cut into wedges. Coarsely chop the walnuts.
11. For assembling, add arugula leaves, apples wedges, cherry tomatoes, cucumber, olives and habanero pepper to a salad bowl.
12. Pour the dressing over veggies and toss well to coat evenly.
13. Top with chopped walnuts and serve.

Spelt grain salad with ginger tahini dressing

NUTRITIONAL VALUES

Amount per Servings, 728 Calories | 48.3 g Fat | 64.1 g Total Carbs | 10.6 g Fiber | 14.1 g Protein

Prep Time	10 min
Cooking Time	30 min
Total Time	40 min
Servings	4 min

INGREDIENTS

- 3 cups spelt grains (washed)
- 2 cups kale leaves
- 4 tbsp olive oil
- 1 cup red pepper (small cubes)
- 1 cup cherry tomatoes (halved)
- ½ cup red onion (chopped)
- 1 cup raisins
- 2 cups tahini sauce
- 2 tsp cayenne pepper
- 1 ½ tbsp dried oregano
- 4 tbsp lime juice
- 2 tbsp grated ginger
- 1 tsp sea salt

DIRECTIONS

1. In a deep pan, boil 6 cups of water and add washed spelt grains. Boil for 30 minutes or until cooked.
2. In a blend, add tahini sauce, lime juice, cayenne pepper, grated ginger, dried oregano, and sea salt. Blend it until smooth.
3. In a bowl, toss the kale leaves with olive oil.
4. Add red peppers, red onion, raisins, cherry tomatoes and spelt grains in the kale.
5. Slowly add tahini dressing according to your taste preference.
6. Drizzle olive oil on top and serve.

Curry Broccoli Salad

NUTRITIONAL VALUES

Amount per Servings, Calories: 182 kcal| Protein: 4g|Carbohydrates: 17g| | Fat: 11g|

Prep Time	15 min
Cook Time	15 min
Total Time	30 min
Servings	6 min

INGREDIENTS

- 1 head broccoli
- 5 tbsp water
- 1/4 cup grapes, halved
- 1/4 cup walnuts, chopped
- Salt & Pepper to Taste
- 1/2 tsp yellow curry powder
- 2 tbsp tahini

DIRECTIONS

1. Cut the broccoli head into florets that are easy to chew.
2. Place in a bowl with grapes and walnuts.
3. Add in a blender: water, curry powder, tahini and mix until dressing is formed.
4. Pour the dressing over the broccoli, grapes and walnuts and mix.
5. Top with salt and pepper and serve.

BREAKFASTS & DESSERTS

Strawberry Ice Cream	**37**
Fruity Yogurt	**38**
Green Detox Smoothie	**39**
Electric Banana cream pie	**40**
Strawberry Banana ice-cream	**41**
Veggie Omelette	**42**
Papaya Breakfast Shake	**43**

Strawberry Ice Cream

NUTRITIONAL VALUES

Amount per Servings, 243 Calories | 18.39 g Fat | 22.04 g Total Carbs | 7.1 g Fiber | 2.67 g Protein

Prep Time	10 min
Cooking Time	8hr
Total Time	8hr-10 min
Servings	2

INGREDIENTS

1 cup strawberries, frozen
1 small avocado, diced
1/4 cup hemp milk
1 Tbsp agave syrup

For Garnishing:
1/2 cup fresh strawberries, chopped

DIRECTIONS

1. In a blender, blend all the ingredients until smooth and creamy.
2. Pour into an air-tight container; cover the surface with a plastic wrap and then with lid.
3. Freeze for at least 8 hours or overnight until firm.
4. Prior to serving, allow to stand at room temperature for about 15 minutes.
5. Scoop out the ice cream into cups. Serve and enjoy!
6. Keep stored in the freezer.

Fruity Yogurt

NUTRITIONAL VALUES

Amount per Servings, 197 Calories | 12.26 g Fat | 23.32 g Total Carbs | 4.8 g Fiber | 2.8 g Protein

Prep Time	15 min
Cooking Time	2hr
Total Time	2hr-15 min
Servings	4

INGREDIENTS

- 1/2 cup strawberries, frozen
- 1/2 blueberries, frozen
- 1/2 cup mangos, chopped
- 1/2 cup walnuts, finely chopped
- 1 avocado, diced
- 1/4 cup spring water
- 3 figs, soaked in water overnight
- 2 **Tbsp** agave syrup
- 1 **Tbsp** lime juice

DIRECTIONS

1. In a blender, blend strawberries, blueberries, avocados, water, figs, agave syrup and lime juice; until smooth.

2. Transfer the mixture to a bowl and stir in chopped mangoes and walnuts.

3. Refrigerate for at least 2 hours.

4. Serve and enjoy!

Green Detox Smoothie

NUTRITIONAL VALUES

Amount per Servings, 777 Calories | 37.88 g Fat | 71.94 g Total Carbs | 10.9 g Fiber | 7.63 g Protein

Prep Time	10 min
Cooking Time	5 min
Total Time	15 min
Servings	2

INGREDIENTS

- 2 cups of hemp seed milk
- 1/2 cup strawberries, sliced
- ½ cup mango, sliced
- 2 bananas, sliced
- 2 dates, pitted
- 1-inch ginger, finely minced
- 1 **Tbsp** agave syrup

DIRECTIONS

1. Gather all the ingredients to a blender and blend on a high speed until smooth.
2. Pour into smoothie glasses, add fancy straws and enjoy!

Electric Banana cream pie

NUTRITIONAL VALUES

Amount per Servings, 568 Calories | 15.5 g Fat | 113.4 g Total Carbs | 12.9 g Fiber | 4.2 g Protein

Prep Time	15 min
Cooking Time	0 min
Total Time	15 min
Servings	4 mint

INGREDIENTS

- 6 Baby or Burro Bananas
- 6 oz Creamed Coconut
- ¾ cup Hemp milk
- 1 ¼ cups Dates (Without pits)
- 1 ¼ cups coconut Flakes (Unsweetened)
- 8 tbsp Agave
- 1 tsp Sea Salt

DIRECTIONS

1. In a food processor, add dates, coconut flakes, 5 tbsp of agave, and 1/8 tsp sea salt. Blend them for 30 to 40 seconds or until combined into a sticky dough consistency.
2. Line a spring form pan with parchment paper and pour out the date mixture.
3. With the help of a spoon spread the mixture out to form an even crust. Refrigerate the crust for 15 to 20 minutes.
4. In a bowl, roughly mash bananas and add creamed coconut, remaining 3 tbsp of agave and hemp milk. With the help of a hand mixer, blend well it until combine.
5. Pour the banana mixture over the crust and smooth the surface out with a spoon.
6. Cover the pie with tin or aluminum foil and refrigerate it for at least 4 hours.
7. Remove the pie from the spring form pan. Sprinkle some coconut flakes and serve chilled.

Strawberry Banana ice-cream

NUTRITIONAL VALUES

Amount per Servings, 100 Calories | 0.3 g Fat | 21 g Total Carbs | 2.6 g Fiber | 0.7 g Protein

Prep Time	10 min
Cooking Time	34 min
Total Time	250 min
Servings	4 min

INGREDIENTS

- 2 cups frozen baby bananas
- 1 cup frozen strawberries
- 1 ½ cups Sea moss gel
- 2 tbsp agave nectar
- 2 tbsp hump seed milk
- Chopped strawberries (garnish)

DIRECTIONS

1. In a power blender or food processor, add all ingredients and blend until creamy and smooth.

2. Eat it as a soft serve or pour the mixture in a container and freeze for 2 to 4 hours until solid.

3. Top with chopped strawberries and serve.

Veggie Omelette

NUTRITIONAL VALUES

Amount per Servings, 247 Calories | 7.8 g Fat | 35.7 g Total Carbs | 10.2 g Fiber | 10.9 g Protein

Prep Time	10 min
Cooking Time	20 min
Total Time	30 min
Servings	4 min

INGREDIENTS

- 1 cup Chickpea flour
- 1 1/3 cup Spring water
- 1 tsp Sea Salt
- 1 tsp Onion Powder
- 1 tsp Sweet Basil
- 1 tsp Oregano
- 1 tsp Cayenne Powder
- 1 cup Onion (Chopped)
- 1 cup Roma Tomato (Diced)
- 1 cup Mushrooms (Chopped)
- 1 cup Green Pepper (Diced)
- 4 tsp Grapeseed oil

DIRECTIONS

1. In a bowl, whisk the chickpea flour, Sea Salt, Onion Powder, Sweet Basil, Oregano, Cayenne Powder.
2. Gradually add spring water and whisk until it gains egg-like consistency.
3. Divide the mixture into 4 equal parts.
4. In a pan, heat 1 tsp of grapeseed oil. Add 2 tbsp of onion, Roma tomatoes, mushroom, and green pepper. Sauté for 2 to 3 minutes.
5. Pour one of the divided flour mixtures over the vegetables and cook for 3 to 4 minutes on medium heat.
6. Flip and cook for another 2 to 3 minutes.
7. Repeat the same with the remaining parts of the vegetables and flour mixture.
8. Serve hot.

Papaya Breakfast Shake

NUTRITIONAL VALUES

Amount per Servings,
Calories: 126kcal | Protein: 1g | Carbohydrate: 30 g | Total Fat: 1 g

Prep Time	1o min
Cook Time	0 min
Total Time	10 min
Servings	2 min

INGREDIENTS

3 cups almond milk

1/2 cup agave nectar

1 tsp sea moss

1/2 cup cold water

1/2 cup fresh or frozen

papaya

DIRECTIONS

1. Blend water and sea moss.

2. Add Papaya, milk, and agave nectar Blend till smooth and serve.

LEGUMES

Garbanzo Burger	**45**
Alkaline Potato Salad styled Garbanzo Beans	**46**
Electric Meatballs	**47**
Chickpea and Mushroom soup with Zucchini noodles	**48**
Chickpea Burger	**49**

Garbanzo Burger

NUTRITIONAL VALUES

Amount per Servings, 489 Calories | 16.46 g Fat | 67.64 g Total Carbs | 13.9 g Fiber | 21.36 g Protein

Prep Time	15 min
Cooking Time	40 min
Total Time	55 min
Servings	4

INGREDIENTS

- 2 cups garbanzo beans
- 8 romaine lettuce leaves
- 1 large bell pepper, diced
- 1 plum tomato, diced (optional)
- 1/2 cup onion, finely chopped
- 1 Tsp dill
- 2 Tsp oregano
- 2 Tsp dried basil
- 1 Tsp thyme
- 1/2 Tsp cayenne pepper
- 3 tsp grapeseed oil

DIRECTIONS

1. Wash the beans and soak them overnight.
2. Next morning, boil them for about 30 minutes or until soft, drain the water and set aside.
3. Place the garbanzo beans and water into the food processor; pulse until there is still texture but most beans have lost their shape. It should hold together when pinched.
4. Transfer the beans into a bowl. Add bell pepper, tomatoes, onion, dill and herbs.
5. Using your clean hands, mix until all the ingredients are evenly combined.
6. Refrigerate the burger mixture for 30 minutes to set.
7. Next, shape the chilled mixture into patties, about 1/2-inch thick.
8. Heat oil in non-stick skillet over medium-high heat.
9. Carefully add the patties to the hot oil and sear each side until nice golden brown, about 3-4 minutes.
10. Serve the patties on lettuce or with any alkaline flatbread.

Alkaline Potato Salad styled Garbanzo Beans

NUTRITIONAL VALUES

Amount per Servings, 381 Calories | 6.6 g Fat | 63.5 g Carbs | 18 g Fiber | 19.8 g Protein

Prep Time	10 min
Cooking Time	30 min
Total Time	40 min
Servings	4 min

INGREDIENTS

- 2 cups Garbanzo Beans
- 1 cup Brazil Nuts
- 1 cup Spring Water (Lukewarm)
- 2 tsp Avocado Oil
- ¼ cup Onions (Chopped)
- ¼ cup Green Peppers (Small cubed)
- ¼ cup Red Peppers (cubes)
- 1 tsp Sea Salt
- 1 ½ tbsp Lime Juice
- ½ tsp Ginger Powder
- ½ tsp Cayenne Powder
- 1 tsp Onion Powder
- 1 tsp Dill
- ½ tsp Sea Moss Gel (Optional)

DIRECTIONS

1. Heat oven to 400F and grease a baking dish with some oil.
2. Using a sharp knife, slice off the top of the bell pepper, reserving the tops.
3. Place the pepper flat end on a cutting board and separate the white inner core, set aside.
4. Heat oil in a large skillet over medium-high heat.
5. Add onion and sauté until slightly golden brown.
6. Add tomatoes, mushrooms, zucchini, squash, onion powder, thyme and salt; cook for about 10 minutes until vegetables are tender.
7. Stir in rice and cook for 5 minutes more.
8. Stir in rice and cook for 5 minutes more.
9. Place the prepared bell peppers into the baking dish.
10. Stuff each pepper with the rice mixture.
11. Place the reserved tops on each stuffed pepper.
12. Drizzle 1 tablespoon of oil on all over the peppers.
13. Cover the dish with aluminum foil and bake for 10 minutes.
14. Remove the foil and bake for 5 minutes more until topping is slightly crisp.
15. Garnish with chopped toasted walnuts and serve.

Electric Meatballs

NUTRITIONAL VALUES

Amount per Servings, 323 Calories | 10.7 g Fat | 46.7 g Total Carbs | 14.9 g Fiber | 14.4 g Protein

Prep Time	15 min
Cooking Time	35 min
Total Time	50 min
Servings	4 min

INGREDIENTS IN

- 1 ¼ cup Mushrooms
- 1 cup Garbanzo beans (Cooked)
- ¼ cup chickpea or garbanzo bean flour
- ¼ cup white onion (Chopped)
- ¼ cup green peppers (Chopped)
- 1 tsp onion powder
- 1 tsp Basil
- 1 tsp Oregano
- 6 green, red, and yellow
- ½ tsp Sage
- ½ tsp Fennel Powder
- ½ tsp Dill
- 1 tsp Sea salt
- ½ tsp Cayenne Powder
- ½ tsp Ginger Powder
- ½ tsp Ground Cloves
- 3 cups Alkaline tomato sauce
- 2 tbsp Grapeseed oil

DIRECTIONS

1. In a food processor, blend all ingredients except grapeseed oil and tomato sauce.
2. Pour the mixture in a bowl and try to make balls. If the mixture is loose, gradually add a few more tablespoons of chickpea or garbanzo flour.
3. In a pan, heat the grapeseed oil to medium heat. Place the meatballs in the pan and cook for 2 minutes on each side.
4. Add tomato sauce to the meatballs and simmer them for 5 to 7 minutes.
5. Serve the meatball hot with flatbread.

Chickpea and Mushroom soup with Zucchini noodles

NUTRITIONAL VALUES

Amount per Servings, 550 Calories | 17.5 g Fat | 80 g Total Carbs | 23.5 g Fiber | 25.7 g Protein

Prep Time	15 min
Cooking Time	25 min
Total Time	40 min
Servings	4 min

INGREDIENTS

- 6 zucchinis
- 8 king oyster mushrooms
- 3 tbsp grapeseed oil
- 1 cup medium white onion (chopped)
- 1 cup red pepper (small cubed)
- 2 tsp sea salt
- 2 tsp onion powder
- 2 tsp cayenne pepper
- 2 cups vegetable broth
- 2 cup drained canned chickpeas
- 1 tsp dried oregano
- 1 tsp dried thyme
- 1 tsp dried basil
- 1 tsp dried tarragon
- Dried parsley (garnish)

DIRECTIONS

1. With a spiraling machine, make zucchini noodles and wash them thoroughly.
2. Wash the king oyster mushroom. Peel them and shred them.
3. In a pot, heat grapeseed oil. Add mushrooms, onions, and red pepper. Cook them until mushroom softens.
4. Add sea salt, onion powder and cayenne powder and mix well.
5. Lower the heat and add vegetable broth, chickpeas, dried oregano, dried thyme, dried basil and dried tarragon.
6. Let the soup simmer for 10 to 15 minutes.
7. Add zucchini noodles to the soup and simmer for 3 to 5 minutes.
8. Serve hot with dried parsley sprinkled on top.

Chickpea Burger

NUTRITIONAL VALUES

Amount per Servings Calories: 130kcal| Protein 6g | |Carbohydrates 20.7g |Total Fat: 3.2g|

Prep Time	20 min
Cook Time	10 min
Total Time	30 min
Servings	40 min

INGREDIENTS

- 1/2 cup Green Peppers, diced
- 1/2 cup Kale, diced
- 2 tsp. Oregano
- 2 tsp. Onion Powder
- 2 tsp. Sea Salt
- 1/2 tsp. Cayenne Powder
- 1/2 cup Spring Water
- Grape Seed Oil
- 1 cup Garbanzo Bean Flour
- 1/2 cup Onions, diced
- 1 Plum Tomato, diced
- 2 tsp. Basil
- 1 tsp. Dill
- 1/2 tsp. Ginger Powder

DIRECTIONS

1. Mix all spices and vegetables in a large bowl and then mix in the flour.
2. Slowly add water and mix it very well.
3. Add more flour if thickness is not good enough.
4. Add oil to the pan and cook the patties on each side for 2-3 minutes over medium heat. Keep turning until both sides are brown.
5. Serve on alkaline flatbread and enjoy the alkaline chickpea burger!

PASTA & GRAINS

Creamy Veggie Pasta	**51**
Electric Macaroni and Cheese	**52**
Electric Walnut pesto Pasta	**53**
Alkaline Creamy Kamut Pasta	**54**
Mexican-Style Quinoa	**55**
Sushi Roll	**56**
Mediterranean Kamut	**57**
Breakfast Skillet	**58**
Cherry Berry Bars	**59**
Alkaline Blackberry Breakfast bars	**60**

Creamy Veggie Pasta

NUTRITIONAL VALUES

Amount per Servings, 627 Calories | 40.98 g Fat | 63.27g Total Carbs | 16.7 g Fiber | 10.38 g Protein

Prep Time	10 min
Cooking Time	25 min
Total Time	35 min
Servings	4

INGREDIENTS

- 2 cups spelt-pasta (you might use other type of pasta, as long as it's approved by Dr. Sebi's Cell Food Nutritional Guide)
- 6 cups spring water
- 1 cup full-fat unsweetened can coconut milk
- 1 cup mushrooms
- 3 cups fresh kale
- 3 Roma tomatoes, chopped
- 2 avocado
- 1 cup fresh basil, chopped
- 1 small onion, finely chopped
- 1/2 cup spring water
- 1/4 cup chickpea flour
- 3 Tbsp grapeseed oil
- 1 Tsp dried oregano
- 1 Tsp dried basil
- 1 Tsp onion powder
- Sea salt and black pepper to taste

DIRECTIONS

1. Bring a large pot of water to a boil.
2. Add a pinch of salt and pasta. Stir well and cook for 10 minutes or a little less than al dente.
3. Slice the avocado in half and using a knife make crosshatch pattern in the avocado flesh or using a tablespoon scoop out the flesh from the avocados into a medium bowl, finely chop them and set aside.
4. Heat a pan over medium-high heat.
5. Add oil and heat until shimmering.
6. Add onion and sauté until slightly golden brown.
7. Stir in chickpea flour, whisking constantly cook for 1 minute or until white froth begins to appear on the top.
8. Immediately pour the coconut milk and water, allow to boil for 2 minutes while stirring.
9. Add oregano, basil, onion powder, salt, and black pepper.
10. Add mushrooms, kale, tomatoes, and basil; reduce the heat and simmer on low for 5-10 minutes, until mixture comes to a boil and thickens.
11. Remove from the heat and let cool at room temperature for about 10 minutes.
12. Meanwhile gather avocado and pasta to a bowl.
13. Pour the creamy mixture on top and toss well to combine.
14. Serve immediately and enjoy.

Electric Macaroni and Cheese

NUTRITIONAL VALUES

Amount per Servings, 749 Calories | 23.8 g Fat | 111.9 g Total Carbs | 19.6 g Fiber | 20 g Protein

Prep Time	40 min
Cooking Time	40 min
Total Time	20 min
Servings	4 mint

INGREDIENTS

- 4 cups Spelt or Kamut pasta
- 1 cup Brazil nuts
- ¼ cup Chickpea flour
- 4 tsp Grapeseed oil
- 1/2 tsp Ground Annatto
- 1 cup Coconut Milk
- 1 cup Spring Water
- 2 tbsp lime juice
- 2 tsp Onion Powder
- 1 tsp Sea Salt

DIRECTIONS

1. Soak the brazil nuts in the water overnight.
2. Boil the pasta until al dente. Drizzle 2 tsp of grapeseed oil over the pasta from avoid sticking together.
3. Preheat the oven 350°F
4. In a blender, add drained brazil nuts, chickpea flour, 2 tsp grapeseed oil, ground annatto, onion powder, lime juice, sea salt, and coconut milk. Blend until smooth.
5. In a bowl, mix pasta and brazil nut mixture.
6. Grease the baking dish with grapeseed oil and pour the pasta in it.
7. Bake the pasta for 25 to 30 minutes.
8. Serve hot.

Electric Walnut Pesto Pasta

NUTRITIONAL VALUES

Amount per Servings, 628 Calories | 45.5 g Fat | 46.5 g Total Carbs | 14.8 g Fiber | 2.1 g Protein

Prep Time	5 min
Cooking Time	10 min
Total Time	15 min
Servings	4 min

INGREDIENTS

- 3/4 lb. spelt pasta
- 2 avocados
- 5 cups fresh basil leaves
- 1 cup walnuts
- 2 tsp grapeseed oil
- Sea salt (to taste)
- 3 tsp lime juice
- 1 cup Black Olives
- 1 cup Cherry tomatoes (Halved)
- ½ cup watercress (Optional)

DIRECTIONS

1. Boil the spelt pasta until al dente then drain them. Drizzle grapeseed oil and toss them. Set aside to cool.
2. In a food processor or blender, blend fresh basil leaves, avocado, walnuts, lime juice and salt until its smooth as a pesto.
3. Add your pesto to cool pasta and toss them well until combine. Add black olives, cherry tomatoes and watercress.
4. Taste and adjust the salt and serve.

Alkaline Creamy Kamut Pasta

NUTRITIONAL VALUES

Amount per Servings, 930 Calories | 42.1 g Fat | 332.3 g Total Carbs | 43.5 g Fiber | 68.3 g Protein

Prep Time	10 min
Cooking Time	30 min
Total Time	40 min
Servings	8 min

INGREDIENTS

- 32 oz spelt pasta
- 4 tbsp grapeseed oil
- 2 tbsp tarragon
- 2 tsp sea salt
- 3 tsp onion powder
- 1 cup white onion (chopped)
- 2 cups mushrooms (sliced)
- Black pepper to taste
- 1 ½ tbsp Chickpea flour
- ½ cup spring water
- 1 cup coconut milk
- 1 tsp dried oregano
- 1 tsp dried thyme
- 1 tsp dried basil

DIRECTIONS

1. Boil the spelt pasta until al dente. Drain and add 1 tbsp of grapeseed oil and toss well.
2. In a bowl, add the drained pasta along with tarragon, 1 tsp sea salt and 1 ½ tsp onion powder. Mix the pasta well and set aside.
3. In a pan, add 1 tbsp on grapeseed oil and heat it to medium heat. Add white onion, mushrooms, 1 tsp sea salt and black pepper. Cook until the mushrooms are golden.
4. Lower the heat and add remaining 2 tbsp of grapeseed oil and chickpea flour, mix is well.
5. Add spring water and coconut milk. Keep stirring to avoid lumps.
6. Add dried oregano, dried thyme and dried basil and cook until thickens.
7. Add in the seasoned pasta and mix well.
8. Serve hot.

Mexican-Style Quinoa

NUTRITIONAL VALUES

Amount per Servings, 423 Calories | 12.43 g Fa | 65.48 g Total Carbs | 9.4 g Fiber | 14.07 g Protein

Prep Time	10 min
Cooking Time	35 min
Total Time	45 min
Servings	4

INGREDIENTS

- 2 cups quinoa
- 4 cups spring water
- 2 large Roma tomatoes, diced
- 1 cup zucchini, chopped
- 1 large red bell pepper, diced
- 1 large green bell pepper, diced
- 1/2 cup onion, chopped
- 2 Tbsp grapeseed oil
- 1 Tbsp onion powder
- 1 Tsp oregano
- 1 Tsp basil
- 1/2 Tsp cayenne pepper
- Sea salt, to taste

DIRECTIONS

1. In a saucepan over medium-low heat, add quinoa and water.
2. Cover with lid and bring to a boil, once the quinoa starts to bubble reduce the heat to low and let it simmer for 20 minutes or until cooked through and the liquid is absorbed.
3. Meanwhile dice the tomatoes, zucchini, bell pepper and onion.
4. Once the quinoa is done, turn off the heat, fluff with a fork and allow to sit for 5 minutes.
5. Heat oil in a large skillet over medium heat.
6. Add onion and sauté until translucent.
7. Immediately stir in tomatoes, zucchini and bell peppers.
8. Add onion powder, oregano, basil, cayenne pepper and salt; stir together.
9. Add cooked quinoa and 1/4 cup of water, cook for 5 minutes more until liquid is cooked off.
10. Stir well and serve warm.

Sushi Roll

NUTRITIONAL VALUES

Amount per Servings, 154 Calories | 7.86 g Fat | 19.93 g Total Carbs | 3.1 g Fiber | 2.87 g Protein

Prep Time	15 min
Cooking Time	10 min
Total Time	25 min
Servings	6

INGREDIENTS

- 4 nori sheets
- 1 cup wild rice, cooked
- 1 cucumber, thinly sliced
- 1 large avocado, sliced into wedges
- 1 ripe mango, sliced into strips
- 1 **Tbsp** sesame seeds plus more for sprinkling
- 1 **Tbsp** olive oil
- 1/2 **Tsp** date sugar
- Sea salt to taste
- 2 **Tbsp** lime juice

DIRECTIONS

1. Combine rice, sesame seeds, lime juice, oil, sugar and salt to a bowl; set aside.
2. In another bowl, combine avocado and mango.
3. Place the nori sheets on a flat surface, shiny side facing down and longest edge facing you.
4. Next arrange the cucumber slices in overlapping rows.
5. Add rice followed by a layer of avocado and mango.
6. Now roll up the nori sheets over the fillings into a tube shape.
7. Transfer the sushi roll to a cutting board and carefully cut them into small slices.
8. Sprinkle the sushi rolls with some sesame seeds and enjoy!

Mediterranean Kamut

NUTRITIONAL VALUES

Amount per Servings, 256 Calories | 9.67 g Fat | 38.63 g Total Carbs | 6.2 g Fiber | 7.33 g Protein

Prep Time	10 min
Cooking Time	1hr-10 min
Total Time	1hr-20 min
Servings	4

INGREDIENTS

- 1 cup kamut
- 3 cups vegetable broth or spring water
- 2-1/2 cup kale, chopped
- 1/2 cup olives, sliced
- 1/2 cup onion, chopped
- Sea salt and freshly ground pepper, to taste
- 2 **Tbsp** lemon juice
- 2 **Tbsp** grapeseed oil

DIRECTIONS

1. Soak kamut in water for up to 8 hours or overnight.
2. Next day, drain the kamut in a colander and set aside.
3. In a medium saucepan over medium-high heat, add broth and kamut; bring to a boil.
4. Once starts to boil, reduce the heat to low, cover and let simmer for about 50-60 minutes until kamut is tender and the liquid is cooked off.
5. When finished cooking, remove from the heat and let cool to room temperature.
6. Meanwhile heat oil in a large skillet over medium heat.
7. Add the onion and cook, stirring until soften, about 5 minutes.
8. Add kale and olives; cook for 5 minutes more.
9. Now stir in the cooked kamut, lemon juice, salt and black pepper, toss to combine.
10. Transfer to a large serving platter and serve warm.

Breakfast Skillet

NUTRITIONAL VALUES

Amount per Servings, 62 Calories | 3.83 g Fat | 6.72 g Total Carbs | 2 g Fiber | 1.81 g Protein

Prep Time	10 min
Cooking Time	35 min
Total Time	45 min
Servings	4

INGREDIENTS

- 1 medium butternut squash, peeled and seeds removed
- 3 cups kale
- 1 cup mushrooms, sliced
- 1 cup tomatoes, chopped
- 1/2 cup onion, finely chopped
- 2 Tsp lime juice
- 1 Tsp onion powder
- 1 Tsp oregano
- 1/2 Tsp thyme
- Sea salt, to taste
- 1/2 cup spring water
- 1 Tbsp avocado oil

DIRECTIONS

1. Cut the squash into cubes and kale into bit-size pieces.
2. Heat a heavy skillet, over medium-low heat. Add oil and heat until shimmering.
3. Place chopped onion into the hot oil and sauté until slightly golden brown.
4. Add in the squash, mushrooms and tomatoes, cook for 5 minutes until tomatoes are softened.
5. Immediately stir in kale, onion powder, oregano, thyme and salt.
6. Pour water, cover and cook until the veggies are softened and nicely browned, about 20 minutes.
7. Add limie juice and stir well.
8. Serve with alkaline flatbread.

Cherry Berry Bars

NUTRITIONAL VALUES

Amount per Servings, 253 Calories | 15.48 g Fat | 23.18 g Total Carbs | 1 g Fiber | 2.15 g Protein

Prep Time	10 min
Cooking Time	25 min
Total Time	35 min
Servings	8

INGREDIENTS

- 1 cup spelt flour
- 1/2 cup blueberries
- 1/2 cup cherries
- 1/4 cup walnuts, finely chopped
- 1/2 cup grapeseed oil
- 1/4 cup agave nectar
- 1/4 Tsp sea salt

DIRECTIONS

1. Preheat oven to 400F. Grease a baking dish with some oil.
2. In a mixing bowl, whisk oil and agave nectar, until fully combined.
3. Stir in flour and salt, fold until well combined.
4. Add in the blueberries, cherries and walnuts, fold again.
5. Transfer the batter into the prepared baking dish and spread evenly with the help of a spatula.
6. Bake for 25 minutes until top is golden brown.
7. Once done, remove from the oven and let cool for 10 minutes.
8. Slice and Serve Warm

Alkaline Blackberry Breakfast bars

NUTRITIONAL VALUES

Amount per Servings, 685 Calories | 111.4 g Fat | 132.1 g Total Carbs | 11.5 g Fiber | 8.9 g Protein

Prep Time	10 min
Cooking Time	30 min
Total Time	40 min
Servings	8 min

INGREDIENTS

- 8 bananas
- 2 cups grapeseed oil
- 1 ½ tbsp agave nectar
- 2 cups quinoa flakes
- 1 cup spelt flour
- 1 tsp sea salt
- 1 cup alkaline blackberry jam

DIRECTIONS

1. Preheat the oven at 400 F. Line a baking tray with parchment paper.
2. In a bowl, peel and smash bananas.
3. Add grapeseed oil, agave nectar, quinoa flakes, spelt flours and sea salt in the bananas and mix well.
4. In a baking tray with parchment, press down the 2/3 of the banana mixture and flatten it out with a spoon.
5. Pour the blackberry jam over it and crumble the remaining 1/3 mixture on the top.
6. Bake for 20 to 30 minutes until golden. Cut in bars while hot and let them cool.
7. Serve with favourite nut milk.

PANCAKES & WRAPS

Savory Jumbo Pancakes	**62**
Banana Pancakes	**63**
Blueberries Muffins	**64**
Alkaline Electric Tacos	**65**
Alkaline Veggie Fajitas	**66**
Alkaline Electric Flatbread	**67**
Alkaline Blueberry Spelt Pancakes	**68**
Squash falafels	**69**
Spelt Strawberry Waffles	**70**
Vegetable Patties	**71**

Savory Jumbo Pancakes

NUTRITIONAL VALUES

Amount per Servings, 444 Calories | 31.03 g Fat | 32.11 g Total Carbs | 6.7 g Fiber | 11.87 g Protein

Prep Time	5 min
Cooking Time	10 min
Total Time	15 min
Servings	2

INGREDIENTS

- 1 cup chickpea flour
- 1/2 cup coconut milk
- 2 Tbsp lime juice
- 1/2 Tsp onion powder
- 1 Tsp oregano
- 1 Tsp thyme
- 2 Tbsp grapeseed oil
- 1/4 Tsp salt

For Garnishing:
- 1 cup cherry tomatoes
- 1/2 cup avocado, sliced
- 1 Tsp onion, diced (optional)
- Pinch of cayenne pepper
- Lime wedges, for serving

DIRECTIONS

1. In a large mixing bowl, except oil combine all the ingredients and mix until well combined.
2. In a pan over a medium heat, add few drops of oil and then 1/4 cup of batter to make a large pancake.
3. Cook for 5 minutes, flip and cook for 5 minutes more until both sides are lightly golden.
4. Repeat until finished with the rest of the batter.
5. Transfer the pancakes to serving plates. Fold in half, top with cherry tomatoes, avocados, and onion.
6. Sprinkle Cayenne pepper and serve with lime wedges.

Banana Pancakes

NUTRITIONAL VALUES

Amount per Servings, 344 Calories | 20.06 g Fat | 35.77 g Total Carbs | 6.3 g Fiber | 8.89 g Protein

Prep Time	5 min
Cooking Time	5 min
Total Time	10 min
Servings	3

INGREDIENTS

- 1 cup chickpea flour
- 1 large banana, mashed
- 3/4 cup unsweetened can coconut milk
- 1-1/2 Tbsp grapeseed oil
- 1 large banana chopped
- 1/2 cup agave syrup
- 1 cup berries

DIRECTIONS

1. Start by adding chickpea flour and mashed banana to a bowl; whisk well.
2. Slowly add coconut milk until you have a thick pancake batter.
3. Heat a nonstick-skillet over medium-high heat.
4. Add oil and heat until hot.
5. Scoop the batter into the pan and cook for 2 minutes until pancake starts to bubble and slightly brown.
6. After 2 minutes flip and cook for 2 minutes more, until browned on both the sides.
7. Stack the pancakes onto a serving plate.
8. Top with berries and sliced bananas.

Blueberry Muffins

NUTRITIONAL VALUES

Amount per Servings, 337 Calories | 15.91 g Fat | 49.63 g Total Carbs | 1.7 g Fiber | 3.32 g Protein

Prep Time	10 min
Cooking Time	25 min
Total Time	35 min
Servings	6

INGREDIENTS

1-1/2 cup spelt flour

1 cup blueberries

3/4 cup agave syrup

4 **Tbsp** grapeseed oil

Dash of sea salt

3/4 cup Perrier water

3/4 cup walnuts, coarsely chopped

1/4 cup raisins

DIRECTIONS

1. Preheat the oven to 375F and line a 6-cup muffin tin with muffin liners.

2. In a mixing bowl, combine flour, walnuts, raisins, and salt.

3. In another mixing bowl, whisk agave and grapeseed oil.

4. Gently fold the dry ingredients into the wet mixture.

5. Pour water and add blueberries, fold again.

6. Spoon the batter into the muffin cups and bake for 20-25 minutes or until a knife inserted in the center comes out clean.

7. Remove from the oven and let cool at room temperature

Alkaline Electric Tacos

NUTRITIONAL VALUES

Amount per Servings, 910 Calories | 43.3 g Fat | 101.9 g Total Carbs | 34.6 g Fiber | 30.9 g Protein

Prep Time	13 min
Cooking Time	0 min
Total Time	15 min
Servings	4 mint

INGREDIENTS

- 2 cup garbanzo beans (Cooked or Canned)
- 3 avocados
- 1 cup tomatoes (Diced)
- ½ cup red onion (Chopped)
- ½ cup red bell pepper (Diced)
- 1 tbsp lime juice
- 1 tbsp Cilantro
- 1 tsp sea salt
- 8 Spelt flour tortillas (Small)
- Lime wedges (garnish)

DIRECTIONS

1. In a bowl, mash avocados and add tomatoes, red onion, red bell pepper, cilantro, sea salt, and lime juice. Mix them well.
2. In a pan, toast spelt tortillas.
3. Make a taco by putting in warm garbanzo beans then guacamole.
4. Serve with a wedge of lime.
5. Stir in rice and cook for 5 minutes more.
6. Place the prepared bell peppers into the baking dish.
7. Stuff each pepper with the rice mixture.
8. Place the reserved tops on each stuffed pepper.
9. Drizzle 1 tablespoon of oil on all over the peppers.
10. Cover the dish with aluminum foil and bake for 10 minutes.
11. Remove the foil and bake for 5 minutes more until topping is slightly crisp.
12. Garnish with chopped toasted walnuts and serve.

Alkaline Veggie Fajitas

NUTRITIONAL VALUES

Amount per Servings, 328 Calories | 15.4 g Fat | 33.9 g Total Carbs | 8.2 g Fiber | 10.7 g Protein

Prep Time	15 min
Cooking Time	10 min
Total Time	25 min
Servings	4 min

INGREDIENTS

- ¾ cups green peppers (Sliced)
- ¾ cups red peppers (Sliced)
- ¾ cups red onions (Sliced)
- ¾ cups white onions (Sliced)
- 2 tsp onion powder
- 2 cups mushrooms (Sliced)
- 1 tsp cayenne pepper
- 2 tsp dried oregano
- 2 tsp dried thyme
- 2 tsp sweet basil
- 2 tbsp lime juice
- 2 tbsp grapeseed oil
- 8 Spelt flour tortillas (Small)
- Lime wedges (For garnish)

DIRECTIONS

1. In a pan, heat grapeseed oil on medium heat.

2. Add mushroom to the pan and cook until soft. Add peppers and onions to the mushroom.

3. Add cayenne pepper, onion powder, dried oregano, dried thyme, and sweet basil and sauté for 5 to 6 minutes.

4. Serve the fajitas with tortillas and lime wedges.

Alkaline Electric Flatbread

NUTRITIONAL VALUES

Amount per Servings, 230 Calories | 3.5 g Fat | 45.1 g Total Carbs | 7.8 g Fiber | 8.4 g Protein

Prep Time	10 min
Cooking Time	20 min
Total Time	30 min
Servings	4 min

INGREDIENTS

- 2 cups Spelt Flour
- 3/4 cup Spring Water
- 2 tsp Grapeseed Oil
- 1/4 tsp Cayenne
- 1 tbsp Sea Salt
- 2 tsp Oregano
- 2 tsp Onion Powder
- 2 tsp basil

DIRECTIONS

1. In a food processor, blend Spelt Flour, sea salt, oregano, basil, onion powder and cayenne until they are combined well.
2. Blend the oil in the mixture. Add ½ cup of water into the flour mixture and blend. Slowly add the water until all comes together in a dough.
3. Dust the workspace with the flour and knead the dough for 4 to 5 minutes. Divide the dough into 4 equal parts.
4. Roll each part into 5-inch circles with the help of a rolling pin.
5. Heat a skillet on medium-high heat. Do not add oil to it.
6. Place in an un-greased skillet on medium-high heat, flipping every 2-3 minutes until done.
7. Serve immediately and enjoy it.

Alkaline Blueberry Spelt Pancakes

NUTRITIONAL VALUES

Amount per Servings, 358 Calories | 6.3 g Fat | 71 g Total Carbs | 8 g Fiber | 9.6 g Protein

Prep Time	10 min
Cooking Time	20 min
Total Time	30 min
Servings	4 min

INGREDIENTS

- 2 cups Spelt Flour
- 1 cup Hemp Milk or Approved Nut Milk
- 2 tbsp Grapeseed
- 1/2 cup Agave
- 2 tbsp Hemp Seeds
- 1 tbsp Grapeseed Oil
- Spring Water
- 1/2 cup Blueberries
- 1/4 tsp Sea Moss

DIRECTIONS

1. In a bowl, mix spelt flour, hemp seeds, agave, sea moss, and grapeseed oil. Mix well.
2. Now mix in 1 cup of hemp milk in the mixture. Slowly, add spring water to adjust the consistency of the batter.
3. Fold the blueberries in the batter.
4. Heat a skillet to medium heat. Lightly coat the skillet with grapeseed oil.
5. Pour the batter into the skillet and let it cook for 3 to 5 minutes. Flip and cook for 3 to 5 minutes more until both sides are lightly golden.
6. Repeat until finished with the rest of the batter.
7. Serve hot and enjoy.

Squash falafels

NUTRITIONAL VALUES

Amount per Servings, 368 Calories | 21.6 g Fat | 115.4 g Total Carbs | 32.9 g Fiber | 35 g Protein

Prep Time	30 min
Cooking Time	30 min
Total Time	60 min
Servings	4 min

INGREDIENTS

- 1 ½ cup butternut squash (peeled and cubed)
- 2 ½ cans of chickpeas (Drained)
- 2 tbsp tahini
- 5 tbsp fresh parsley
- 5 tbsp fresh coriander
- 3 tbsp onion powder
- 1 ½ tbsp cayenne
- 1 white medium onion (Chopped)
- 3/4 cup chickpea flour
- sea salt (to taste)
- 2 tbsp grapeseed oil
- 3 tbsp dried dill
- 3 tbsp dried oregano

DIRECTIONS

1. Steam the butternut squash for 20 minutes or until fork-tender. Set aside to cool at room temperature.
2. In a food processor, add drained chickpeas, squash, onion, cayenne, fresh coriander, fresh parsley, onion powder, dried dill, dried oregano, tahini, grapeseed oil and chickpea flour. Pulse until just combined; otherwise, it will be too soft to handle.
3. Preheat the oven at 400 F and line a baking tray with parchment paper.
4. Scoop out the mixture into balls and place them on the baking tray.
5. Bake them for 20 to 30 minutes until crispy outside
6. Serve them hot with yogurt.

Spelt Strawberry Waffles

NUTRITIONAL VALUES

Amount per Servings, Calories: 227.7 kcal | protein: 22 g | carbohydrates: 11.7 g | fat: 9.3 g |

Prep Time	1o min
Cook Time	10 min
Total Time	20 min
Servings	10 min

INGREDIENTS

- 1 Cup spelt flour
- 1/2 cup almond milk
- 1/4 cup water
- 1/4 cup of agave nectar
- 1 tsp vanilla extract
- 6 strawberries cut into small pieces
- Vinegar
- Butter
- Eggs
- Maple Syrup
- 1 tsp Salt
- Baking Powder
- Soy Milk

DIRECTIONS

1. Whisk the spelled flour, whole meal flour, baking powder and salt. Whisk the mixture containing soy milk and vinegar, butter, eggs and vanilla in a separate large bowl. Add flour to the wet mix and stir until just combined. Let it rest for 15 minutes.

2. While the waffle mixture is at rest, make the compote. In a small saucepan, add the strawberries, 1/8 cup water, maple syrup and place over a medium heat. Cook until the mixture thickens, about 10 minutes. Remove from heat and stir in the lemon zest and juice.

3. Heat a waffle maker according to the manufacturer's instructions. Cook until golden and crispy, and then top with strawberry compote.

Vegetable Patties

NUTRITIONAL VALUES

Amount per Servings
Calories: 129kcal | Protein: 4g | Carbohydrate: 15g | |Total Fat: 6 g |

Prep Time	25 min
Cook Time	60 min
Total Time	85 min
Servings	8 min

INGREDIENTS

- 1/2 red and green peppers chopped
- 1 medium yellow onion chopped fine
- Spring Water
- Kamut Flour
- 1 pinch of African red pepper
- 3 tbs olive oil
- 1 bunch of broccoli chopped fine
- 1 bunch of kale greens cut fine
- 2 chayote squash diced
- 1/4 cup sea moss powder

DIRECTIONS

1. Heat skillet with 3 tbs olive oil
2. Add onion, bell pepper, chayote squash, African red pepper and ground cumin, sauté 2-3 minutes
3. Add broccoli and kale and simmer for 10-12 minutes.

Preparation for Kamut flour:

1. Mix sea moss with enough flour and water to make dough.
2. Roll out on floured board cut into 10" diameter circles.
3. Place cooked vegetables 1/2 of circle.
4. Fold other half to cover the vegetables.
5. Use a fork to pinch the edges closed.
6. Place patties on lightly greased baking sheet and bake 20-30 minutes or until golden brown.

1001 DAYS OF MEAL SCHEDULES

I hope you are enjoying the recipes and that by now you are making and cooking delicious canned foods to enjoy with all your family and friends.

So you never run out of ideas and you continue cooking every day without having to worry what to cook and when, I have devised a varied and diversified 1001 day meal plan for your meals.

This way you will be able to cook for over 3 years non-stop without ever having to wonder what to choose. Just check the ingredients you need for the week, head to the grocery store and start cooking from the very first day!

Every schedule includes three meals to prepare for every day, ensuring you cook varied meals to never, ever getting tired of your canning and preserving skills. Enjoy!

WEEK 1	MONDAY	TUESDAY	WEDNESDAY	THURSDAY	FRIDAY	SATURDAY	SUNDAY
MEAL 1	Squash Falafels	Blueberries Muffins	Alkaline Veggie Fajitas	Vegetable Patties	Fruity Yogurt	Savory Jumbo Pancakes	Vegetable Patties
MEAL 2	Sesame Turnip Greens	Classic Hummus	Stuffed Bell Pepper	Sesame Turnip Greens	Sesame Turnip Greens	Home-Style Okra	Home-Style Okra
MEAL 3	Chickpea Burger	Alkaline Potato Salad	Lettuce Cups	Mac & Cheese	Pepper Relish	Alkaline Potato Salad	Corn Relish

WEEK 2	MONDAY	TUESDAY	WEDNESDAY	THURSDAY	FRIDAY	SATURDAY	SUNDAY
MEAL 1	Strawberry Ice Cream	Squash Falafels	Lettuce Cups	Squash Falafels	Stuffed Avocado Salad	Vegetable Patties	Squash Falafels
MEAL 2	Wild Rice Stuffed Peppers	Classic Hummus	Kale Pesto	Butternut Soup	Fruit Skewers	Fruit Skewers	Spinach Bowl
MEAL 3	Corn Relish	Alkaline Potato Salad	Chickpea and Mushroom	Mac & Cheese	Mediterranean Kamut	Papaya Breakfast Shake	Alkaline Potato Salad

WEEK 3	MONDAY	TUESDAY	WEDNESDAY	THURSDAY	FRIDAY	SATURDAY	SUNDAY
MEAL 1	Alkaline Electric Flatbread	Alkaline Electric Tacos	Banana Pancakes	Banana Pancakes	Lettuce Cups	Lettuce Cups	Blueberries Muffins
MEAL 2	Roasted Okra	Wild Rice Stuffed Peppers	Vegetable Mushroom Sauce	Spicy Soup	Walnut Breakfast	Spicy Soup	The Greatest Greens
MEAL 3	Electric Meatballs	Garbanzo Burger	Pepper Relish	Alkaline Potato Salad	Corn Relish	Rose Petals Honey	Papaya Breakfast Shake

WEEK 4	MONDAY	TUESDAY	WEDNESDAY	THURSDAY	FRIDAY	SATURDAY	SUNDAY
MEAL 1	Alkaline Veggie Fajitas	Spelt Strawberry Waffles	Squash Falafels	Squash Falafels	Vegetable Patties	Herbed Mushroom Stew	Alkaline Veggie Fajitas
MEAL 2	Stuffed Bell Pepper	Kale Pesto	Spinach Bowl	Stir-Fried Watercress	Vegetable Mushroom Sauce	Stuffed Bell Pepper	Home-Style Okra
MEAL 3	Papaya Breakfast Shake	Mexican-Style Quinoa	Mexican-Style Quinoa	Chickpea Burger	Papaya Breakfast Shake	Strawberry ice-cream	Rose Petals Honey

WEEK 5	MONDAY	TUESDAY	WEDNESDAY	THURSDAY	FRIDAY	SATURDAY	SUNDAY
MEAL 1	Strawberry Ice Cream	Alkaline Veggie Fajitas	Cucumber Dill Salad	Vegetable Patties	Blueberries Muffins	Savory Jumbo Pancakes	Lettuce Cups
MEAL 2	Stuffed Bell Pepper	Classic Hummus	Classic Hummus	Kale Pesto	Alkaline Zucchini Coleslaw	Wild Rice Stuffed Peppers	Vegan Apple Turnovers
MEAL 3	Creamy Veggie Pasta	Breakfast Skillet	Papaya Breakfast Shake	Corn Relish	Pepper Relish	Canned Boneless Chicken	Canned Boneless Chicken

WEEK 6	MONDAY	TUESDAY	WEDNESDAY	THURSDAY	FRIDAY	SATURDAY	SUNDAY
MEAL 1	Blueberries Muffins	Strawberry Ice Cream	Alkaline Veggie Fajitas	Savory Jumbo Pancakes	Savory Jumbo Pancakes	Alkaline Electric Tacos	Spelt Pancakes
MEAL 2	Bone Broth	Alkaline Zucchini Coleslaw	Sesame Turnip Greens	Butternut Soup	Roasted Okra	Kale Pesto	The Greatest Greens
MEAL 3	Pepper Relish	Pepper Relish	Mexican-Style Quinoa	Rose Petals Honey	Mexican-Style Quinoa	Chickpea and Mushroom	Creamy Veggie Pasta

WEEK 7	MONDAY	TUESDAY	WEDNESDAY	THURSDAY	FRIDAY	SATURDAY	SUNDAY
MEAL 1	Alkaline Electric Flatbread	Curry Broccoli Salad	Alkaline Electric Tacos	Banana Pancakes	Herbed Mushroom Stew	Savory Jumbo Pancakes	Spelt grain salad
MEAL 2	Vegetable Mushroom Sauce	Caramalized Strawberry ice-cream	Vegetable Mushroom Sauce	The Greatest Greens	Spinach Bowl	Roasted Okra	Spinach Bowl
MEAL 3	Veggie Omelette	Pepper Relish	Corn Relish	Chickpea Burger	Garbanzo Burger	Chickpea and Mushroom	Chickpea and Mushroom

WEEK 8	MONDAY	TUESDAY	WEDNESDAY	THURSDAY	FRIDAY	SATURDAY	SUNDAY
MEAL 1	Stuffed Avocado Salad	Spelt Strawberry Waffles	Lettuce Cups	Fruity Yogurt	Alkaline Veggie Fajitas	Spelt Pancakes	Spelt Strawberry Waffles
MEAL 2	Spicy Soup	Walnut Breakfast	The Greatest Greens	Alkaline Zucchini Coleslaw	Vegan Apple Turnovers	Butternut Soup	Stuffed Bell Pepper
MEAL 3	Veggie Omelette	Mac & Cheese	Rose Petals Honey	Chickpea and Mushroom	Mexican-Style Quinoa	Mac & Cheese	Corn Relish

WEEK 9	MONDAY	TUESDAY	WEDNESDAY	THURSDAY	FRIDAY	SATURDAY	SUNDAY
MEAL 1	Alkaline Electric Flatbread	Strawberry Ice Cream	Squash Falafels	Savory Jumbo Pancakes	Stuffed Avocado Salad	Curry Broccoli Salad	Vegetable Patties
MEAL 2	Vegetable Mushroom Sauce	Bone Broth	Classic Hummus	Stuffed Bell Pepper	Caramalized Strawberry ice-cream	Sesame Turnip Greens	Wild Rice Stuffed Peppers
MEAL 3	Mexican-Style Quinoa	Rose Petals Honey	Lettuce Cups	Canned Boneless Chicken	Mediterranean Kamut	Electric Meatballs	Rose Petals Honey

WEEK 10	MONDAY	TUESDAY	WEDNESDAY	THURSDAY	FRIDAY	SATURDAY	SUNDAY
MEAL 1	Herbed Mushroom Stew	Cinnamon Peach Jam	Herbed Mushroom Stew	Stuffed Avocado Salad	Spelt Pancakes	Banana Pancakes	Spelt Pancakes
MEAL 2	Spinach Bowl	Vegetable Mushroom Sauce	Classic Hummus	Spinach Bowl	Zucchini Fritters	Zucchini Fritters	Spinach Bowl
MEAL 3	Walnut Pesto Pasta	Mac & Cheese	Garbanzo Burger	Canned Boneless Chicken	Papaya Breakfast Shake	Mexican-Style Quinoa	Chickpea Burger

WEEK 11	MONDAY	TUESDAY	WEDNESDAY	THURSDAY	FRIDAY	SATURDAY	SUNDAY
MEAL 1	Strawberry Ice Cream	Savory Jumbo Pancakes	Banana Pancakes	Herbed Mushroom Stew	Cucumber Dill Salad	Alkaline Veggie Fajitas	Alkaline Veggie Fajitas
MEAL 2	Kale Pesto	Bone Broth	Walnut Breakfast	Vegan Apple Turnovers	Sesame Turnip Greens	Alkaline Zucchini Coleslaw	Butternut Soup
MEAL 3	Chickpea Burger	Veggie Omelette	Creamy Veggie Pasta	Papaya Breakfast Shake	Chickpea and Mushroom	Walnut Pesto Pasta	Mediterranean Kamut

WEEK 12	MONDAY	TUESDAY	WEDNESDAY	THURSDAY	FRIDAY	SATURDAY	SUNDAY
MEAL 1	Cinnamon Peach Jam	Cinnamon Peach Jam	Spelt grain salad	Alkaline Electric Flatbread	Banana Pancakes	Alkaline Electric Flatbread	Curry Broccoli Salad
MEAL 2	Stir-Fried Watercress	Spinach Bowl	Bone Broth	Caramalized Strawberry ice-cream	The Greatest Greens	Alkaline Zucchini Coleslaw	Caramalized Strawberry ice-cream
MEAL 3	Mac & Cheese	Papaya Breakfast Shake	Veggie Omelette	Papaya Breakfast Shake	Pepper Relish	Creamy Veggie Pasta	Walnut Pesto Pasta

WEEK 13	MONDAY	TUESDAY	WEDNESDAY	THURSDAY	FRIDAY	SATURDAY	SUNDAY
MEAL 1	Banana Pancakes	Alkaline Veggie Fajitas	Arugula Salad	Stuffed Avocado Salad	Squash Falafels	Alkaline Electric Tacos	Curry Broccoli Salad
MEAL 2	Caramalized Strawberry ice-cream	Sesame Turnip Greens	Stuffed Bell Pepper	Classic Hummus	Kale Pesto	Classic Hummus	Zucchini Fritters
MEAL 3	Mac & Cheese	Corn Relish	Lettuce Cups	Corn Relish	Veggie Omelette	Breakfast Skillet	Garbanzo Burger

WEEK 14	MONDAY	TUESDAY	WEDNESDAY	THURSDAY	FRIDAY	SATURDAY	SUNDAY
MEAL 1	Curry Broccoli Salad	Fruity Yogurt	Banana Pancakes	Spelt grain salad	Savory Jumbo Pancakes	Stuffed Avocado Salad	Herbed Mushroom Stew
MEAL 2	Spicy Soup	Caramalized Strawberry ice-cream	Fruit Skewers	Stir-Fried Watercress	Bone Broth	Home-Style Okra	Vegetable Mushroom Sauce
MEAL 3	Strawberry ice-cream	Papaya Breakfast Shake	Veggie Omelette	Pepper Relish	Pepper Relish	Breakfast Skillet	Chickpea Burger

WEEK 15	MONDAY	TUESDAY	WEDNESDAY	THURSDAY	FRIDAY	SATURDAY	SUNDAY
MEAL 1	Squash Falafels	Savory Jumbo Pancakes	Alkaline Veggie Fajitas	Curry Broccoli Salad	Banana Pancakes	Alkaline Electric Flatbread	Alkaline Electric Tacos
MEAL 2	Caramalized Strawberry ice-cream	Classic Hummus	Bone Broth	Walnut Breakfast	Vegetable Mushroom Sauce	Spinach Bowl	Zucchini Fritters
MEAL 3	Corn Relish	Strawberry ice-cream	Creamy Kamut Pasta	Creamy Veggie Pasta	Strawberry ice-cream	Veggie Omelette	Breakfast Skillet

WEEK 16	MONDAY	TUESDAY	WEDNESDAY	THURSDAY	FRIDAY	SATURDAY	SUNDAY
MEAL 1	Alkaline Electric Tacos	Herbed Mushroom Stew	Vegetable Patties	Alkaline Veggie Fajitas	Savory Jumbo Pancakes	Squash Falafels	Savory Jumbo Pancakes
MEAL 2	Zucchini Fritters	Vegetable Mushroom Sauce	Kale Pesto	Vegan Apple Turnovers	Spinach Bowl	Bone Broth	Stir-Fried Watercress
MEAL 3	Veggie Omelette	Walnut Pesto Pasta	Chickpea and Mushroom	Corn Relish	Walnut Pesto Pasta	Papaya Breakfast Shake	Veggie Omelette

WEEK 17	MONDAY	TUESDAY	WEDNESDAY	THURSDAY	FRIDAY	SATURDAY	SUNDAY
MEAL 1	Savory Jumbo Pancakes	Cinnamon Peach Jam	Vegetable Patties	Spelt Pancakes	Alkaline Electric Flatbread	Alkaline Electric Flatbread	Banana Pancakes
MEAL 2	Spinach Bowl	Spinach Bowl	Spinach Bowl	Roasted Okra	Vegetable Mushroom Sauce	Wild Rice Stuffed Peppers	Vegan Apple Turnovers
MEAL 3	Canned Boneless Chicken	Electric Meatballs	Corn Relish	Alkaline Potato Salad	Corn Relish	Papaya Breakfast Shake	Pepper Relish

WEEK 18	MONDAY	TUESDAY	WEDNESDAY	THURSDAY	FRIDAY	SATURDAY	SUNDAY
MEAL 1	Banana Pancakes	Arugula Salad	Alkaline Veggie Fajitas	Alkaline Electric Tacos	Squash Falafels	Spelt Strawberry Waffles	Arugula Salad
MEAL 2	Home-Style Okra	Stuffed Bell Pepper	Caramalized Strawberry ice-cream	Spicy Soup	Caramalized Strawberry ice-cream	Zucchini Fritters	Sesame Turnip Greens
MEAL 3	Chickpea and Mushroom	Creamy Veggie Pasta	Canned Boneless Chicken	Veggie Omelette	Strawberry ice-cream	Corn Relish	Papaya Breakfast Shake

WEEK 19	MONDAY	TUESDAY	WEDNESDAY	THURSDAY	FRIDAY	SATURDAY	SUNDAY
MEAL 1	Strawberry Ice Cream	Alkaline Veggie Fajitas	Spelt Pancakes	Strawberry Ice Cream	Lettuce Cups	Vegetable Patties	Cinnamon Peach Jam
MEAL 2	Kale Pesto	Walnut Breakfast	Stir-Fried Watercress	Vegetable Mushroom Sauce	Home-Style Okra	Bone Broth	Home-Style Okra
MEAL 3	Creamy Veggie Pasta	Canned Boneless Chicken	Mediterranean Kamut	Pepper Relish	Alkaline Potato Salad	Mexican-Style Quinoa	Breakfast Skillet

WEEK 20	MONDAY	TUESDAY	WEDNESDAY	THURSDAY	FRIDAY	SATURDAY	SUNDAY
MEAL 1	Blueberries Muffins	Spelt grain salad	Cinnamon Peach Jam	Fruity Yogurt	Alkaline Veggie Fajitas	Fruity Yogurt	Fruity Yogurt
MEAL 2	Stir-Fried Watercress	Vegetable Mushroom Sauce	Caramalized Strawberry ice-cream	Vegan Apple Turnovers	Stir-Fried Watercress	Zucchini Fritters	Spicy Soup
MEAL 3	Creamy Kamut Pasta	Rose Petals Honey	Lettuce Cups	Mexican-Style Quinoa	Electric Meatballs	Corn Relish	Breakfast Skillet

WEEK 21	MONDAY	TUESDAY	WEDNESDAY	THURSDAY	FRIDAY	SATURDAY	SUNDAY
MEAL 1	Alkaline Veggie Fajitas	Spelt Strawberry Waffles	Strawberry Ice Cream	Blueberries Muffins	Vegetable Patties	Savory Jumbo Pancakes	Alkaline Electric Flatbread
MEAL 2	Zucchini Fritters	Stuffed Bell Pepper	Spicy Soup	Spicy Soup	The Greatest Greens	Spicy Soup	Fruit Skewers
MEAL 3	Walnut Pesto Pasta	Chickpea Burger	Walnut Pesto Pasta	Canned Boneless Chicken	Veggie Omelette	Breakfast Skillet	Papaya Breakfast Shake

WEEK 22	MONDAY	TUESDAY	WEDNESDAY	THURSDAY	FRIDAY	SATURDAY	SUNDAY
MEAL 1	Spelt grain salad	Blueberries Muffins	Vegetable Patties	Arugula Salad	Spelt Strawberry Waffles	Blueberries Muffins	Banana Pancakes
MEAL 2	Home-Style Okra	Spicy Soup	Caramalized Strawberry ice-cream	Vegan Apple Turnovers	Classic Hummus	Home-Style Okra	Spinach Bowl
MEAL 3	Electric Meatballs	Mediterranean Kamut	Rose Petals Honey	Creamy Veggie Pasta	Lettuce Cups	Lettuce Cups	Mediterranean Kamut

WEEK 23	MONDAY	TUESDAY	WEDNESDAY	THURSDAY	FRIDAY	SATURDAY	SUNDAY
MEAL 1	Spelt Strawberry Waffles	Cucumber Dill Salad	Alkaline Electric Tacos	Savory Jumbo Pancakes	Blueberries Muffins	Cinnamon Peach Jam	Stuffed Avocado Salad
MEAL 2	Walnut Breakfast	Classic Hummus	Fruit Skewers	Stuffed Bell Pepper	Vegetable Mushroom Sauce	Roasted Okra	Home-Style Okra
MEAL 3	Rose Petals Honey	Creamy Veggie Pasta	Mediterranean Kamut	Chickpea and Mushroom	Chickpea Burger	Rose Petals Honey	Veggie Omelette

WEEK 24	MONDAY	TUESDAY	WEDNESDAY	THURSDAY	FRIDAY	SATURDAY	SUNDAY
MEAL 1	Squash Falafels	Lettuce Cups	Fruity Yogurt	Cucumber Dill Salad	Fruity Yogurt	Alkaline Electric Flatbread	Lettuce Cups
MEAL 2	Walnut Breakfast	Stuffed Bell Pepper	Walnut Breakfast	Fruit Skewers	Butternut Soup	Roasted Okra	Spinach Bowl
MEAL 3	Walnut Pesto Pasta	Mexican-Style Quinoa	Mexican-Style Quinoa	Mediterranean Kamut	Papaya Breakfast Shake	Mac & Cheese	Canned Boneless Chicken

WEEK 25	MONDAY	TUESDAY	WEDNESDAY	THURSDAY	FRIDAY	SATURDAY	SUNDAY
MEAL 1	Alkaline Electric Tacos	Alkaline Veggie Fajitas	Blueberries Muffins	Herbed Mushroom Stew	Strawberry Ice Cream	Vegetable Patties	Cinnamon Peach Jam
MEAL 2	Zucchini Fritters	Sesame Turnip Greens	The Greatest Greens	Sesame Turnip Greens	Vegan Apple Turnovers	Stuffed Bell Pepper	Sesame Turnip Greens
MEAL 3	Electric Meatballs	Walnut Pesto Pasta	Pepper Relish	Chickpea and Mushroom	Alkaline Potato Salad	Chickpea Burger	Chickpea Burger

WEEK 26	MONDAY	TUESDAY	WEDNESDAY	THURSDAY	FRIDAY	SATURDAY	SUNDAY
MEAL 1	Arugula Salad	Alkaline Veggie Fajitas	Arugula Salad	Lettuce Cups	Vegetable Patties	Alkaline Veggie Fajitas	Banana Pancakes
MEAL 2	Fruit Skewers	Vegan Apple Turnovers	Caramalized Strawberry ice-cream	Caramalized Strawberry ice-cream	Caramalized Strawberry ice-cream	Zucchini Fritters	Fruit Skewers
MEAL 3	Canned Boneless Chicken	Corn Relish	Alkaline Potato Salad	Creamy Kamut Pasta	Walnut Pesto Pasta	Garbanzo Burger	Creamy Kamut Pasta

WEEK 27	MONDAY	TUESDAY	WEDNESDAY	THURSDAY	FRIDAY	SATURDAY	SUNDAY
MEAL 1	Spelt Pancakes	Cinnamon Peach Jam	Banana Pancakes	Fruity Yogurt	Blueberries Muffins	Curry Broccoli Salad	Cucumber Dill Salad
MEAL 2	Fruit Skewers	Classic Hummus	Bone Broth	Vegan Apple Turnovers	Butternut Soup	Spinach Bowl	Alkaline Zucchini Coleslaw
MEAL 3	Mexican-Style Quinoa	Rose Petals Honey	Electric Meatballs	Pepper Relish	Rose Petals Honey	Mac & Cheese	Rose Petals Honey

WEEK 28	MONDAY	TUESDAY	WEDNESDAY	THURSDAY	FRIDAY	SATURDAY	SUNDAY
MEAL 1	Alkaline Electric Flatbread	Cinnamon Peach Jam	Blueberries Muffins	Stuffed Avocado Salad	Alkaline Electric Flatbread	Vegetable Patties	Stuffed Avocado Salad
MEAL 2	Home-Style Okra	Walnut Breakfast	Roasted Okra	The Greatest Greens	Caramalized Strawberry ice-cream	Stuffed Bell Pepper	Stir-Fried Watercress
MEAL 3	Papaya Breakfast Shake	Chickpea Burger	Veggie Omelette	Corn Relish	Corn Relish	Creamy Veggie Pasta	Chickpea and Mushroom

WEEK 29	MONDAY	TUESDAY	WEDNESDAY	THURSDAY	FRIDAY	SATURDAY	SUNDAY
MEAL 1	Stuffed Avocado Salad	Fruity Yogurt	Cinnamon Peach Jam	Savory Jumbo Pancakes	Vegetable Patties	Alkaline Electric Tacos	Spelt Pancakes
MEAL 2	Wild Rice Stuffed Peppers	Spinach Bowl	Vegetable Mushroom Sauce	Classic Hummus	Zucchini Fritters	Stuffed Bell Pepper	Butternut Soup
MEAL 3	Lettuce Cups	Chickpea Burger	Mediterranean Kamut	Garbanzo Burger	Walnut Pesto Pasta	Chickpea Burger	Alkaline Potato Salad

WEEK 30	MONDAY	TUESDAY	WEDNESDAY	THURSDAY	FRIDAY	SATURDAY	SUNDAY
MEAL 1	Fruity Yogurt	Alkaline Veggie Fajitas	Curry Broccoli Salad	Blueberries Muffins	Arugula Salad	Savory Jumbo Pancakes	Herbed Mushroom Stew
MEAL 2	Fruit Skewers	Walnut Breakfast	Walnut Breakfast	Zucchini Fritters	Alkaline Zucchini Coleslaw	Spinach Bowl	Sesame Turnip Greens
MEAL 3	Veggie Omelette	Papaya Breakfast Shake	Pepper Relish	Strawberry ice-cream	Chickpea Burger	Corn Relish	Walnut Pesto Pasta

WEEK 31	MONDAY	TUESDAY	WEDNESDAY	THURSDAY	FRIDAY	SATURDAY	SUNDAY
MEAL 1	Spelt Pancakes	Spelt Strawberry Waffles	Banana Pancakes	Stuffed Avocado Salad	Curry Broccoli Salad	Spelt Pancakes	Spelt Pancakes
MEAL 2	Roasted Okra	Butternut Soup	Vegetable Mushroom Sauce	The Greatest Greens	Home-Style Okra	The Greatest Greens	Kale Pesto
MEAL 3	Canned Boneless Chicken	Strawberry ice-cream	Lettuce Cups	Creamy Kamut Pasta	Walnut Pesto Pasta	Garbanzo Burger	Creamy Kamut Pasta

WEEK 32	MONDAY	TUESDAY	WEDNESDAY	THURSDAY	FRIDAY	SATURDAY	SUNDAY
MEAL 1	Arugula Salad	Vegetable Patties	Cucumber Dill Salad	Strawberry Ice Cream	Curry Broccoli Salad	Lettuce Cups	Banana Pancakes
MEAL 2	Caramalized Strawberry ice-cream	Alkaline Zucchini Coleslaw	Butternut Soup	Stuffed Bell Pepper	The Greatest Greens	Stir-Fried Watercress	Classic Hummus
MEAL 3	Breakfast Skillet	Canned Boneless Chicken	Walnut Pesto Pasta	Mac & Cheese	Walnut Pesto Pasta	Pepper Relish	Lettuce Cups

WEEK 33	MONDAY	TUESDAY	WEDNESDAY	THURSDAY	FRIDAY	SATURDAY	SUNDAY
MEAL 1	Spelt grain salad	Strawberry Ice Cream	Alkaline Electric Tacos	Banana Pancakes	Herbed Mushroom Stew	Arugula Salad	Curry Broccoli Salad
MEAL 2	Kale Pesto	Walnut Breakfast	Spinach Bowl	Stir-Fried Watercress	Kale Pesto	Stuffed Bell Pepper	Sesame Turnip Greens
MEAL 3	Mexican-Style Quinoa	Lettuce Cups	Creamy Veggie Pasta	Corn Relish	Chickpea Burger	Mexican-Style Quinoa	Creamy Veggie Pasta

WEEK 34	MONDAY	TUESDAY	WEDNESDAY	THURSDAY	FRIDAY	SATURDAY	SUNDAY
MEAL 1	Spelt Pancakes	Blueberries Muffins	Alkaline Veggie Fajitas	Cucumber Dill Salad	Herbed Mushroom Stew	Spelt Pancakes	Vegetable Patties
MEAL 2	Kale Pesto	Butternut Soup	Zucchini Fritters	Alkaline Zucchini Coleslaw	Vegetable Mushroom Sauce	Fruit Skewers	Alkaline Zucchini Coleslaw
MEAL 3	Strawberry ice-cream	Breakfast Skillet	Electric Meatballs	Pepper Relish	Veggie Omelette	Papaya Breakfast Shake	Breakfast Skillet

WEEK 35	MONDAY	TUESDAY	WEDNESDAY	THURSDAY	FRIDAY	SATURDAY	SUNDAY
MEAL 1	Alkaline Electric Flatbread	Squash Falafels	Alkaline Electric Flatbread	Squash Falafels	Spelt Strawberry Waffles	Alkaline Veggie Fajitas	Banana Pancakes
MEAL 2	Zucchini Fritters	Stir-Fried Watercress	Vegan Apple Turnovers	Sesame Turnip Greens	Wild Rice Stuffed Peppers	Vegetable Mushroom Sauce	Kale Pesto
MEAL 3	Canned Boneless Chicken	Garbanzo Burger	Mediterranean Kamut	Alkaline Potato Salad	Rose Petals Honey	Creamy Veggie Pasta	Mediterranean Kamut

WEEK 36	MONDAY	TUESDAY	WEDNESDAY	THURSDAY	FRIDAY	SATURDAY	SUNDAY
MEAL 1	Cucumber Dill Salad	Arugula Salad	Alkaline Electric Flatbread	Alkaline Electric Flatbread	Alkaline Electric Tacos	Savory Jumbo Pancakes	Curry Broccoli Salad
MEAL 2	Stir-Fried Watercress	Spicy Soup	Fruit Skewers	Fruit Skewers	Vegan Apple Turnovers	Spinach Bowl	Vegetable Mushroom Sauce
MEAL 3	Creamy Veggie Pasta	Mac & Cheese	Mac & Cheese	Papaya Breakfast Shake	Pepper Relish	Garbanzo Burger	Mac & Cheese

WEEK 37	MONDAY	TUESDAY	WEDNESDAY	THURSDAY	FRIDAY	SATURDAY	SUNDAY
MEAL 1	Stuffed Avocado Salad	Lettuce Cups	Vegetable Patties	Alkaline Electric Flatbread	Alkaline Electric Tacos	Stuffed Avocado Salad	Cinnamon Peach Jam
MEAL 2	Classic Hummus	The Greatest Greens	Zucchini Fritters	Kale Pesto	Spicy Soup	Spicy Soup	The Greatest Greens
MEAL 3	Chickpea and Mushroom	Walnut Pesto Pasta	Papaya Breakfast Shake	Garbanzo Burger	Canned Boneless Chicken	Breakfast Skillet	Corn Relish

WEEK 38	MONDAY	TUESDAY	WEDNESDAY	THURSDAY	FRIDAY	SATURDAY	SUNDAY
MEAL 1	Herbed Mushroom Stew	Alkaline Electric Flatbread	Spelt Pancakes	Lettuce Cups	Banana Pancakes	Stuffed Avocado Salad	Arugula Salad
MEAL 2	Classic Hummus	Sesame Turnip Greens	Vegan Apple Turnovers	Fruit Skewers	Vegan Apple Turnovers	Roasted Okra	Spinach Bowl
MEAL 3	Breakfast Skillet	Mediterranean Kamut	Alkaline Potato Salad	Rose Petals Honey	Mediterranean Kamut	Alkaline Potato Salad	Breakfast Skillet

WEEK 39	MONDAY	TUESDAY	WEDNESDAY	THURSDAY	FRIDAY	SATURDAY	SUNDAY
MEAL 1	Curry Broccoli Salad	Arugula Salad	Alkaline Veggie Fajitas	Arugula Salad	Cucumber Dill Salad	Fruity Yogurt	Alkaline Electric Flatbread
MEAL 2	Zucchini Fritters	Roasted Okra	Home-Style Okra	Spicy Soup	Spinach Bowl	Stir-Fried Watercress	Classic Hummus
MEAL 3	Creamy Veggie Pasta	Chickpea and Mushroom	Chickpea Burger	Mac & Cheese	Strawberry ice-cream	Strawberry ice-cream	Mediterranean Kamut

WEEK 40	MONDAY	TUESDAY	WEDNESDAY	THURSDAY	FRIDAY	SATURDAY	SUNDAY
MEAL 1	Arugula Salad	Alkaline Veggie Fajitas	Cinnamon Peach Jam	Stuffed Avocado Salad	Herbed Mushroom Stew	Cucumber Dill Salad	Vegetable Patties
MEAL 2	Home-Style Okra	Bone Broth	Walnut Breakfast	Home-Style Okra	Stuffed Bell Pepper	Bone Broth	Stuffed Bell Pepper
MEAL 3	Mexican-Style Quinoa	Papaya Breakfast Shake	Chickpea Burger	Corn Relish	Chickpea and Mushroom	Chickpea Burger	Mediterranean Kamut

WEEK 41	MONDAY	TUESDAY	WEDNESDAY	THURSDAY	FRIDAY	SATURDAY	SUNDAY
MEAL 1	Strawberry Ice Cream	Spelt Pancakes	Banana Pancakes	Banana Pancakes	Squash Falafels	Squash Falafels	Arugula Salad
MEAL 2	Caramalized Strawberry ice-cream	Fruit Skewers	Caramalized Strawberry ice-cream	Vegetable Mushroom Sauce	Spicy Soup	Stuffed Bell Pepper	Stuffed Bell Pepper
MEAL 3	Creamy Veggie Pasta	Pepper Relish	Pepper Relish	Mediterranean Kamut	Mediterranean Kamut	Veggie Omelette	Lettuce Cups

WEEK 42	MONDAY	TUESDAY	WEDNESDAY	THURSDAY	FRIDAY	SATURDAY	SUNDAY
MEAL 1	Arugula Salad	Cucumber Dill Salad	Alkaline Veggie Fajitas	Stuffed Avocado Salad	Cucumber Dill Salad	Strawberry Ice Cream	Alkaline Veggie Fajitas
MEAL 2	Wild Rice Stuffed Peppers	Wild Rice Stuffed Peppers	The Greatest Greens	Kale Pesto	The Greatest Greens	Kale Pesto	Spicy Soup
MEAL 3	Mediterranean Kamut	Breakfast Skillet	Corn Relish	Papaya Breakfast Shake	Mexican-Style Quinoa	Creamy Kamut Pasta	Veggie Omelette

WEEK 43	MONDAY	TUESDAY	WEDNESDAY	THURSDAY	FRIDAY	SATURDAY	SUNDAY
MEAL 1	Savory Jumbo Pancakes	Lettuce Cups	Blueberries Muffins	Lettuce Cups	Blueberries Muffins	Spelt grain salad	Cucumber Dill Salad
MEAL 2	Kale Pesto	Caramalized Strawberry ice-cream	Spicy Soup	Spinach Bowl	Butternut Soup	Stir-Fried Watercress	Stir-Fried Watercress
MEAL 3	Creamy Veggie Pasta	Breakfast Skillet	Mac & Cheese	Lettuce Cups	Breakfast Skillet	Walnut Pesto Pasta	Garbanzo Burger

WEEK 44	MONDAY	TUESDAY	WEDNESDAY	THURSDAY	FRIDAY	SATURDAY	SUNDAY
MEAL 1	Squash Falafels	Vegetable Patties	Alkaline Electric Tacos	Alkaline Veggie Fajitas	Banana Pancakes	Squash Falafels	Spelt grain salad
MEAL 2	Walnut Breakfast	The Greatest Greens	Vegetable Mushroom Sauce	Alkaline Zucchini Coleslaw	Fruit Skewers	Kale Pesto	Classic Hummus
MEAL 3	Mexican-Style Quinoa	Corn Relish	Chickpea Burger	Breakfast Skillet	Chickpea Burger	Mac & Cheese	Veggie Omelette

WEEK 45	MONDAY	TUESDAY	WEDNESDAY	THURSDAY	FRIDAY	SATURDAY	SUNDAY
MEAL 1	Savory Jumbo Pancakes	Cucumber Dill Salad	Squash Falafels	Cucumber Dill Salad	Strawberry Ice Cream	Alkaline Veggie Fajitas	Vegetable Patties
MEAL 2	Stir-Fried Watercress	Caramalized Strawberry ice-cream	Alkaline Zucchini Coleslaw	Classic Hummus	Caramalized Strawberry ice-cream	Classic Hummus	Stir-Fried Watercress
MEAL 3	Walnut Pesto Pasta	Mexican-Style Quinoa	Pepper Relish	Veggie Omelette	Mexican-Style Quinoa	Electric Meatballs	Pepper Relish

WEEK 46	MONDAY	TUESDAY	WEDNESDAY	THURSDAY	FRIDAY	SATURDAY	SUNDAY
MEAL 1	Spelt Strawberry Waffles	Herbed Mushroom Stew	Cucumber Dill Salad	Cucumber Dill Salad	Alkaline Electric Flatbread	Savory Jumbo Pancakes	Squash Falafels
MEAL 2	Roasted Okra	Zucchini Fritters	Sesame Turnip Greens	Alkaline Zucchini Coleslaw	Vegetable Mushroom Sauce	Wild Rice Stuffed Peppers	The Greatest Greens
MEAL 3	Creamy Kamut Pasta	Corn Relish	Canned Boneless Chicken	Garbanzo Burger	Mac & Cheese	Corn Relish	Creamy Veggie Pasta

WEEK 47	MONDAY	TUESDAY	WEDNESDAY	THURSDAY	FRIDAY	SATURDAY	SUNDAY
MEAL 1	Spelt grain salad	Curry Broccoli Salad	Spelt Pancakes	Alkaline Electric Flatbread	Alkaline Electric Flatbread	Stuffed Avocado Salad	Strawberry Ice Cream
MEAL 2	Bone Broth	Stuffed Bell Pepper	Wild Rice Stuffed Peppers	Caramalized Strawberry ice-cream	Spicy Soup	Zucchini Fritters	The Greatest Greens
MEAL 3	Garbanzo Burger	Lettuce Cups	Veggie Omelette	Electric Meatballs	Garbanzo Burger	Chickpea and Mushroom	Pepper Relish

WEEK 48	MONDAY	TUESDAY	WEDNESDAY	THURSDAY	FRIDAY	SATURDAY	SUNDAY
MEAL 1	Blueberries Muffins	Cinnamon Peach Jam	Herbed Mushroom Stew	Cinnamon Peach Jam	Squash Falafels	Alkaline Veggie Fajitas	Cinnamon Peach Jam
MEAL 2	Spicy Soup	Stir-Fried Watercress	Zucchini Fritters	Alkaline Zucchini Coleslaw	The Greatest Greens	Vegan Apple Turnovers	Home-Style Okra
MEAL 3	Alkaline Potato Salad	Papaya Breakfast Shake	Veggie Omelette	Strawberry ice-cream	Canned Boneless Chicken	Garbanzo Burger	Pepper Relish

WEEK 49	MONDAY	TUESDAY	WEDNESDAY	THURSDAY	FRIDAY	SATURDAY	SUNDAY
MEAL 1	Herbed Mushroom Stew	Alkaline Electric Flatbread	Stuffed Avocado Salad	Fruity Yogurt	Blueberries Muffins	Lettuce Cups	Squash Falafels
MEAL 2	Butternut Soup	The Greatest Greens	Sesame Turnip Greens	Roasted Okra	Spinach Bowl	Spicy Soup	Caramalized Strawberry ice-cream
MEAL 3	Creamy Kamut Pasta	Corn Relish	Veggie Omelette	Alkaline Potato Salad	Chickpea and Mushroom	Breakfast Skillet	Mexican-Style Quinoa

WEEK 50	MONDAY	TUESDAY	WEDNESDAY	THURSDAY	FRIDAY	SATURDAY	SUNDAY
MEAL 1	Herbed Mushroom Stew	Cucumber Dill Salad	Savory Jumbo Pancakes	Squash Falafels	Vegetable Patties	Alkaline Electric Flatbread	Banana Pancakes
MEAL 2	Kale Pesto	Spinach Bowl	Caramalized Strawberry ice-cream	Fruit Skewers	Vegan Apple Turnovers	Bone Broth	Vegetable Mushroom Sauce
MEAL 3	Mediterranean Kamut	Papaya Breakfast Shake	Creamy Veggie Pasta	Mexican-Style Quinoa	Alkaline Potato Salad	Lettuce Cups	Walnut Pesto Pasta

WEEK 51	MONDAY	TUESDAY	WEDNESDAY	THURSDAY	FRIDAY	SATURDAY	SUNDAY
MEAL 1	Squash Falafels	Cinnamon Peach Jam	Vegetable Patties	Spelt Strawberry Waffles	Cucumber Dill Salad	Fruity Yogurt	Banana Pancakes
MEAL 2	Classic Hummus	Spinach Bowl	Roasted Okra	Kale Pesto	Caramalized Strawberry ice-cream	Fruit Skewers	Spinach Bowl
MEAL 3	Rose Petals Honey	Creamy Kamut Pasta	Alkaline Potato Salad	Garbanzo Burger	Chickpea and Mushroom	Lettuce Cups	Walnut Pesto Pasta

WEEK 52	MONDAY	TUESDAY	WEDNESDAY	THURSDAY	FRIDAY	SATURDAY	SUNDAY
MEAL 1	Herbed Mushroom Stew	Spelt Strawberry Waffles	Alkaline Veggie Fajitas	Cinnamon Peach Jam	Cucumber Dill Salad	Vegetable Patties	Spelt Pancakes
MEAL 2	Fruit Skewers	Vegan Apple Turnovers	Stuffed Bell Pepper	Butternut Soup	Spicy Soup	Caramalized Strawberry ice-cream	Vegetable Mushroom Sauce
MEAL 3	Garbanzo Burger	Mediterranean Kamut	Mexican-Style Quinoa	Breakfast Skillet	Mexican-Style Quinoa	Chickpea Burger	Papaya Breakfast Shake

WEEK 53	MONDAY	TUESDAY	WEDNESDAY	THURSDAY	FRIDAY	SATURDAY	SUNDAY
MEAL 1	Stuffed Avocado Salad	Curry Broccoli Salad	Savory Jumbo Pancakes	Fruity Yogurt	Blueberries Muffins	Banana Pancakes	Cucumber Dill Salad
MEAL 2	Roasted Okra	Home-Style Okra	Kale Pesto	Roasted Okra	Roasted Okra	Spicy Soup	Fruit Skewers
MEAL 3	Veggie Omelette	Pepper Relish	Veggie Omelette	Electric Meatballs	Chickpea and Mushroom	Mexican-Style Quinoa	Strawberry ice-cream

WEEK 54	MONDAY	TUESDAY	WEDNESDAY	THURSDAY	FRIDAY	SATURDAY	SUNDAY
MEAL 1	Vegetable Patties	Alkaline Electric Tacos	Cucumber Dill Salad	Spelt Strawberry Waffles	Vegetable Patties	Arugula Salad	Alkaline Electric Flatbread
MEAL 2	Vegetable Mushroom Sauce	Sesame Turnip Greens	Kale Pesto	Spinach Bowl	Zucchini Fritters	Roasted Okra	Caramalized Strawberry ice-cream
MEAL 3	Veggie Omelette	Veggie Omelette	Creamy Veggie Pasta	Chickpea Burger	Alkaline Potato Salad	Corn Relish	Chickpea Burger

WEEK 55	MONDAY	TUESDAY	WEDNESDAY	THURSDAY	FRIDAY	SATURDAY	SUNDAY
MEAL 1	Cucumber Dill Salad	Spelt grain salad	Stuffed Avocado Salad	Vegetable Patties	Fruity Yogurt	Arugula Salad	Banana Pancakes
MEAL 2	Vegetable Mushroom Sauce	Bone Broth	Vegetable Mushroom Sauce	Spinach Bowl	Butternut Soup	Spinach Bowl	Bone Broth
MEAL 3	Mediterranean Kamut	Breakfast Skillet	Chickpea Burger	Alkaline Potato Salad	Pepper Relish	Pepper Relish	Electric Meatballs

WEEK 56	MONDAY	TUESDAY	WEDNESDAY	THURSDAY	FRIDAY	SATURDAY	SUNDAY
MEAL 1	Stuffed Avocado Salad	Spelt grain salad	Arugula Salad	Arugula Salad	Herbed Mushroom Stew	Cucumber Dill Salad	Spelt Strawberry Waffles
MEAL 2	Kale Pesto	Stuffed Bell Pepper	Spicy Soup	Stuffed Bell Pepper	Caramalized Strawberry ice-cream	Alkaline Zucchini Coleslaw	Alkaline Zucchini Coleslaw
MEAL 3	Corn Relish	Mexican-Style Quinoa	Mediterranean Kamut	Chickpea and Mushroom	Chickpea and Mushroom	Veggie Omelette	Creamy Kamut Pasta

WEEK 57	MONDAY	TUESDAY	WEDNESDAY	THURSDAY	FRIDAY	SATURDAY	SUNDAY
MEAL 1	Alkaline Electric Tacos	Alkaline Veggie Fajitas	Spelt grain salad	Cucumber Dill Salad	Arugula Salad	Vegetable Patties	Fruity Yogurt
MEAL 2	Vegetable Mushroom Sauce	Alkaline Zucchini Coleslaw	Kale Pesto	Caramalized Strawberry ice-cream	Stir-Fried Watercress	Home-Style Okra	Caramalized Strawberry ice-cream
MEAL 3	Creamy Kamut Pasta	Alkaline Potato Salad	Strawberry ice-cream	Alkaline Potato Salad	Breakfast Skillet	Strawberry ice-cream	Mac & Cheese

WEEK 58	MONDAY	TUESDAY	WEDNESDAY	THURSDAY	FRIDAY	SATURDAY	SUNDAY
MEAL 1	Alkaline Electric Tacos	Lettuce Cups	Alkaline Electric Flatbread	Spelt grain salad	Alkaline Veggie Fajitas	Stuffed Avocado Salad	Cinnamon Peach Jam
MEAL 2	Zucchini Fritters	Sesame Turnip Greens	Vegan Apple Turnovers	Spinach Bowl	Stuffed Bell Pepper	The Greatest Greens	Walnut Breakfast
MEAL 3	Electric Meatballs	Mexican-Style Quinoa	Breakfast Skillet	Lettuce Cups	Strawberry ice-cream	Mediterranean Kamut	Garbanzo Burger

WEEK 59	MONDAY	TUESDAY	WEDNESDAY	THURSDAY	FRIDAY	SATURDAY	SUNDAY
MEAL 1	Cinnamon Peach Jam	Vegetable Patties	Spelt grain salad	Lettuce Cups	Lettuce Cups	Lettuce Cups	Fruity Yogurt
MEAL 2	Zucchini Fritters	Wild Rice Stuffed Peppers	Spinach Bowl	The Greatest Greens	Wild Rice Stuffed Peppers	Spinach Bowl	Caramalized Strawberry ice-cream
MEAL 3	Alkaline Potato Salad	Chickpea and Mushroom	Strawberry ice-cream	Walnut Pesto Pasta	Electric Meatballs	Creamy Kamut Pasta	Chickpea Burger

WEEK 60	MONDAY	TUESDAY	WEDNESDAY	THURSDAY	FRIDAY	SATURDAY	SUNDAY
MEAL 1	Savory Jumbo Pancakes	Blueberries Muffins	Spelt Strawberry Waffles	Alkaline Electric Tacos	Alkaline Electric Tacos	Fruity Yogurt	Lettuce Cups
MEAL 2	Zucchini Fritters	Walnut Breakfast	Roasted Okra	Classic Hummus	Classic Hummus	Kale Pesto	Sesame Turnip Greens
MEAL 3	Walnut Pesto Pasta	Canned Boneless Chicken	Mediterranean Kamut	Electric Meatballs	Walnut Pesto Pasta	Breakfast Skillet	Electric Meatballs

WEEK 61	MONDAY	TUESDAY	WEDNESDAY	THURSDAY	FRIDAY	SATURDAY	SUNDAY
MEAL 1	Spelt Pancakes	Savory Jumbo Pancakes	Cucumber Dill Salad	Spelt Pancakes	Spelt Strawberry Waffles	Blueberries Muffins	Cinnamon Peach Jam
MEAL 2	Home-Style Okra	Caramalized Strawberry ice-cream	Spicy Soup	Alkaline Zucchini Coleslaw	Sesame Turnip Greens	Vegetable Mushroom Sauce	Fruit Skewers
MEAL 3	Veggie Omelette	Creamy Veggie Pasta	Veggie Omelette	Breakfast Skillet	Creamy Veggie Pasta	Pepper Relish	Pepper Relish

WEEK 62	MONDAY	TUESDAY	WEDNESDAY	THURSDAY	FRIDAY	SATURDAY	SUNDAY
MEAL 1	Strawberry Ice Cream	Herbed Mushroom Stew	Spelt Strawberry Waffles	Alkaline Electric Flatbread	Cucumber Dill Salad	Arugula Salad	Lettuce Cups
MEAL 2	Stuffed Bell Pepper	Classic Hummus	Wild Rice Stuffed Peppers	Classic Hummus	The Greatest Greens	Wild Rice Stuffed Peppers	Zucchini Fritters
MEAL 3	Creamy Kamut Pasta	Lettuce Cups	Corn Relish	Alkaline Potato Salad	Lettuce Cups	Chickpea Burger	Rose Petals Honey

WEEK 63	MONDAY	TUESDAY	WEDNESDAY	THURSDAY	FRIDAY	SATURDAY	SUNDAY
MEAL 1	Squash Falafels	Alkaline Electric Tacos	Strawberry Ice Cream	Savory Jumbo Pancakes	Herbed Mushroom Stew	Cinnamon Peach Jam	Blueberries Muffins
MEAL 2	Kale Pesto	Vegetable Mushroom Sauce	Stuffed Bell Pepper	Bone Broth	Spicy Soup	Bone Broth	Roasted Okra
MEAL 3	Walnut Pesto Pasta	Strawberry ice-cream	Chickpea and Mushroom	Papaya Breakfast Shake	Breakfast Skillet	Garbanzo Burger	Alkaline Potato Salad

WEEK 64	MONDAY	TUESDAY	WEDNESDAY	THURSDAY	FRIDAY	SATURDAY	SUNDAY
MEAL 1	Alkaline Electric Tacos	Curry Broccoli Salad	Alkaline Veggie Fajitas	Arugula Salad	Squash Falafels	Squash Falafels	Fruity Yogurt
MEAL 2	Vegetable Mushroom Sauce	Stuffed Bell Pepper	Alkaline Zucchini Coleslaw	Vegetable Mushroom Sauce	Vegan Apple Turnovers	Home-Style Okra	Classic Hummus
MEAL 3	Mexican-Style Quinoa	Pepper Relish	Mediterranean Kamut	Walnut Pesto Pasta	Mac & Cheese	Breakfast Skillet	Walnut Pesto Pasta

WEEK 65	MONDAY	TUESDAY	WEDNESDAY	THURSDAY	FRIDAY	SATURDAY	SUNDAY
MEAL 1	Curry Broccoli Salad	Alkaline Electric Flatbread	Spelt grain salad	Cucumber Dill Salad	Blueberries Muffins	Blueberries Muffins	Alkaline Electric Flatbread
MEAL 2	Spicy Soup	Home-Style Okra	Roasted Okra	Stuffed Bell Pepper	Zucchini Fritters	The Greatest Greens	Roasted Okra
MEAL 3	Canned Boneless Chicken	Rose Petals Honey	Creamy Veggie Pasta	Breakfast Skillet	Strawberry ice-cream	Walnut Pesto Pasta	Corn Relish

WEEK 66	MONDAY	TUESDAY	WEDNESDAY	THURSDAY	FRIDAY	SATURDAY	SUNDAY
MEAL 1	Spelt Strawberry Waffles	Vegetable Patties	Arugula Salad	Cucumber Dill Salad	Spelt Pancakes	Strawberry Ice Cream	Fruity Yogurt
MEAL 2	Fruit Skewers	Bone Broth	Stuffed Bell Pepper	The Greatest Greens	Zucchini Fritters	Sesame Turnip Greens	Stuffed Bell Pepper
MEAL 3	Chickpea and Mushroom	Pepper Relish	Strawberry ice-cream	Strawberry ice-cream	Strawberry ice-cream	Papaya Breakfast Shake	Mexican-Style Quinoa

WEEK 67	MONDAY	TUESDAY	WEDNESDAY	THURSDAY	FRIDAY	SATURDAY	SUNDAY
MEAL 1	Curry Broccoli Salad	Cinnamon Peach Jam	Alkaline Electric Tacos	Squash Falafels	Strawberry Ice Cream	Spelt Strawberry Waffles	Savory Jumbo Pancakes
MEAL 2	Home-Style Okra	Stuffed Bell Pepper	Wild Rice Stuffed Peppers	Butternut Soup	Kale Pesto	Spinach Bowl	Home-Style Okra
MEAL 3	Creamy Kamut Pasta	Garbanzo Burger	Creamy Kamut Pasta	Canned Boneless Chicken	Creamy Veggie Pasta	Breakfast Skillet	Rose Petals Honey

WEEK 68	MONDAY	TUESDAY	WEDNESDAY	THURSDAY	FRIDAY	SATURDAY	SUNDAY
MEAL 1	Vegetable Patties	Savory Jumbo Pancakes	Alkaline Veggie Fajitas	Arugula Salad	Spelt Pancakes	Curry Broccoli Salad	Spelt Pancakes
MEAL 2	Caramalized Strawberry ice-cream	Wild Rice Stuffed Peppers	Stir-Fried Watercress	Zucchini Fritters	Vegetable Mushroom Sauce	Fruit Skewers	Home-Style Okra
MEAL 3	Alkaline Potato Salad	Chickpea and Mushroom	Creamy Kamut Pasta	Papaya Breakfast Shake	Electric Meatballs	Mac & Cheese	Walnut Pesto Pasta

WEEK 69	MONDAY	TUESDAY	WEDNESDAY	THURSDAY	FRIDAY	SATURDAY	SUNDAY
MEAL 1	Vegetable Patties	Arugula Salad	Cinnamon Peach Jam	Stuffed Avocado Salad	Stuffed Avocado Salad	Stuffed Avocado Salad	Spelt grain salad
MEAL 2	Stuffed Bell Pepper	Walnut Breakfast	Vegan Apple Turnovers	Walnut Breakfast	Caramalized Strawberry ice-cream	Roasted Okra	Spinach Bowl
MEAL 3	Alkaline Potato Salad	Canned Boneless Chicken	Walnut Pesto Pasta	Breakfast Skillet	Canned Boneless Chicken	Mac & Cheese	Corn Relish

WEEK 70	MONDAY	TUESDAY	WEDNESDAY	THURSDAY	FRIDAY	SATURDAY	SUNDAY
MEAL 1	Spelt Pancakes	Savory Jumbo Pancakes	Alkaline Veggie Fajitas	Spelt grain salad	Squash Falafels	Alkaline Veggie Fajitas	Alkaline Electric Tacos
MEAL 2	Spicy Soup	Stuffed Bell Pepper	Stir-Fried Watercress	Bone Broth	Sesame Turnip Greens	Wild Rice Stuffed Peppers	Vegan Apple Turnovers
MEAL 3	Walnut Pesto Pasta	Veggie Omelette	Veggie Omelette	Mac & Cheese	Chickpea Burger	Veggie Omelette	Rose Petals Honey

WEEK 71	MONDAY	TUESDAY	WEDNESDAY	THURSDAY	FRIDAY	SATURDAY	SUNDAY
MEAL 1	Alkaline Electric Tacos	Squash Falafels	Spelt grain salad	Vegetable Patties	Spelt Strawberry Waffles	Arugula Salad	Strawberry Ice Cream
MEAL 2	Caramalized Strawberry ice-cream	Vegetable Mushroom Sauce	Walnut Breakfast	Zucchini Fritters	Home-Style Okra	Sesame Turnip Greens	Alkaline Zucchini Coleslaw
MEAL 3	Strawberry ice-cream	Lettuce Cups	Rose Petals Honey	Corn Relish	Lettuce Cups	Creamy Kamut Pasta	Chickpea Burger

WEEK 72	MONDAY	TUESDAY	WEDNESDAY	THURSDAY	FRIDAY	SATURDAY	SUNDAY
MEAL 1	Arugula Salad	Fruity Yogurt	Herbed Mushroom Stew	Banana Pancakes	Lettuce Cups	Alkaline Veggie Fajitas	Blueberries Muffins
MEAL 2	Walnut Breakfast	Spinach Bowl	Walnut Breakfast	Walnut Breakfast	Wild Rice Stuffed Peppers	Zucchini Fritters	Stir-Fried Watercress
MEAL 3	Mexican-Style Quinoa	Lettuce Cups	Electric Meatballs	Walnut Pesto Pasta	Canned Boneless Chicken	Garbanzo Burger	Chickpea Burger

WEEK 73	MONDAY	TUESDAY	WEDNESDAY	THURSDAY	FRIDAY	SATURDAY	SUNDAY
MEAL 1	Cinnamon Peach Jam	Fruity Yogurt	Fruity Yogurt	Banana Pancakes	Squash Falafels	Savory Jumbo Pancakes	Herbed Mushroom Stew
MEAL 2	Kale Pesto	Classic Hummus	Fruit Skewers	Vegan Apple Turnovers	Fruit Skewers	Stuffed Bell Pepper	Spinach Bowl
MEAL 3	Garbanzo Burger	Chickpea and Mushroom	Canned Boneless Chicken	Corn Relish	Walnut Pesto Pasta	Garbanzo Burger	Garbanzo Burger

WEEK 74	MONDAY	TUESDAY	WEDNESDAY	THURSDAY	FRIDAY	SATURDAY	SUNDAY
MEAL 1	Stuffed Avocado Salad	Arugula Salad	Alkaline Veggie Fajitas	Strawberry Ice Cream	Alkaline Electric Flatbread	Strawberry Ice Cream	Arugula Salad
MEAL 2	Spicy Soup	Stir-Fried Watercress	Walnut Breakfast	Zucchini Fritters	The Greatest Greens	Spicy Soup	Classic Hummus
MEAL 3	Creamy Veggie Pasta	Corn Relish	Corn Relish	Creamy Kamut Pasta	Garbanzo Burger	Veggie Omelette	Creamy Kamut Pasta

WEEK 75	MONDAY	TUESDAY	WEDNESDAY	THURSDAY	FRIDAY	SATURDAY	SUNDAY
MEAL 1	Spelt Pancakes	Alkaline Electric Tacos	Herbed Mushroom Stew	Strawberry Ice Cream	Spelt Pancakes	Cinnamon Peach Jam	Alkaline Electric Tacos
MEAL 2	Sesame Turnip Greens	Stuffed Bell Pepper	Classic Hummus	Zucchini Fritters	Roasted Okra	Classic Hummus	Caramalized Strawberry ice-cream
MEAL 3	Chickpea Burger	Chickpea Burger	Electric Meatballs	Chickpea and Mushroom	Creamy Kamut Pasta	Creamy Veggie Pasta	Breakfast Skillet

WEEK 76	MONDAY	TUESDAY	WEDNESDAY	THURSDAY	FRIDAY	SATURDAY	SUNDAY
MEAL 1	Blueberries Muffins	Cucumber Dill Salad	Fruity Yogurt	Strawberry Ice Cream	Cucumber Dill Salad	Savory Jumbo Pancakes	Alkaline Electric Tacos
MEAL 2	Sesame Turnip Greens	Zucchini Fritters	Wild Rice Stuffed Peppers	Wild Rice Stuffed Peppers	Butternut Soup	Caramalized Strawberry ice-cream	Home-Style Okra
MEAL 3	Pepper Relish	Rose Petals Honey	Mexican-Style Quinoa	Canned Boneless Chicken	Pepper Relish	Chickpea Burger	Breakfast Skillet

WEEK 77	MONDAY	TUESDAY	WEDNESDAY	THURSDAY	FRIDAY	SATURDAY	SUNDAY
MEAL 1	Spelt Pancakes	Strawberry Ice Cream	Stuffed Avocado Salad	Fruity Yogurt	Squash Falafels	Alkaline Electric Tacos	Spelt grain salad
MEAL 2	Roasted Okra	Spicy Soup	Caramalized Strawberry ice-cream	Roasted Okra	Spinach Bowl	Vegan Apple Turnovers	Spinach Bowl
MEAL 3	Papaya Breakfast Shake	Alkaline Potato Salad	Lettuce Cups	Mac & Cheese	Mediterranean Kamut	Chickpea Burger	Papaya Breakfast Shake

WEEK 78	MONDAY	TUESDAY	WEDNESDAY	THURSDAY	FRIDAY	SATURDAY	SUNDAY
MEAL 1	Squash Falafels	Alkaline Electric Flatbread	Savory Jumbo Pancakes	Squash Falafels	Curry Broccoli Salad	Stuffed Avocado Salad	Blueberries Muffins
MEAL 2	Zucchini Fritters	Classic Hummus	Vegan Apple Turnovers	Roasted Okra	Vegetable Mushroom Sauce	Bone Broth	Stir-Fried Watercress
MEAL 3	Corn Relish	Garbanzo Burger	Pepper Relish	Mexican-Style Quinoa	Pepper Relish	Corn Relish	Garbanzo Burger

WEEK 79	MONDAY	TUESDAY	WEDNESDAY	THURSDAY	FRIDAY	SATURDAY	SUNDAY
MEAL 1	Curry Broccoli Salad	Squash Falafels	Cinnamon Peach Jam	Lettuce Cups	Cucumber Dill Salad	Alkaline Electric Tacos	Spelt grain salad
MEAL 2	The Greatest Greens	Spicy Soup	Fruit Skewers	Fruit Skewers	Kale Pesto	Fruit Skewers	Spicy Soup
MEAL 3	Rose Petals Honey	Veggie Omelette	Creamy Kamut Pasta	Mac & Cheese	Papaya Breakfast Shake	Creamy Veggie Pasta	Mac & Cheese

WEEK 80	MONDAY	TUESDAY	WEDNESDAY	THURSDAY	FRIDAY	SATURDAY	SUNDAY
MEAL 1	Strawberry Ice Cream	Alkaline Electric Tacos	Herbed Mushroom Stew	Cinnamon Peach Jam	Banana Pancakes	Cinnamon Peach Jam	Alkaline Veggie Fajitas
MEAL 2	Classic Hummus	Sesame Turnip Greens	Zucchini Fritters	Home-Style Okra	Butternut Soup	Zucchini Fritters	Home-Style Okra
MEAL 3	Canned Boneless Chicken	Walnut Pesto Pasta	Electric Meatballs	Creamy Kamut Pasta	Lettuce Cups	Mediterranean Kamut	Alkaline Potato Salad

WEEK 81	MONDAY	TUESDAY	WEDNESDAY	THURSDAY	FRIDAY	SATURDAY	SUNDAY
MEAL 1	Spelt Pancakes	Cucumber Dill Salad	Cucumber Dill Salad	Curry Broccoli Salad	Spelt grain salad	Fruity Yogurt	Alkaline Veggie Fajitas
MEAL 2	Classic Hummus	Vegetable Mushroom Sauce	Spicy Soup	Bone Broth	The Greatest Greens	Wild Rice Stuffed Peppers	Spinach Bowl
MEAL 3	Walnut Pesto Pasta	Alkaline Potato Salad	Corn Relish	Mediterranean Kamut	Rose Petals Honey	Mexican-Style Quinoa	Creamy Veggie Pasta

WEEK 82	MONDAY	TUESDAY	WEDNESDAY	THURSDAY	FRIDAY	SATURDAY	SUNDAY
MEAL 1	Lettuce Cups	Strawberry Ice Cream	Vegetable Patties	Vegetable Patties	Spelt grain salad	Spelt grain salad	Vegetable Patties
MEAL 2	Spicy Soup	Spicy Soup	Bone Broth	Roasted Okra	Home-Style Okra	Stuffed Bell Pepper	Roasted Okra
MEAL 3	Electric Meatballs	Lettuce Cups	Electric Meatballs	Canned Boneless Chicken	Chickpea and Mushroom	Rose Petals Honey	Veggie Omelette

WEEK 83	MONDAY	TUESDAY	WEDNESDAY	THURSDAY	FRIDAY	SATURDAY	SUNDAY
MEAL 1	Squash Falafels	Cucumber Dill Salad	Spelt Pancakes	Alkaline Electric Flatbread	Spelt grain salad	Alkaline Veggie Fajitas	Arugula Salad
MEAL 2	Bone Broth	Home-Style Okra	Sesame Turnip Greens	Walnut Breakfast	Caramalized Strawberry ice-cream	Classic Hummus	Walnut Breakfast
MEAL 3	Veggie Omelette	Canned Boneless Chicken	Mediterranean Kamut	Creamy Kamut Pasta	Rose Petals Honey	Lettuce Cups	Mac & Cheese

WEEK 84	MONDAY	TUESDAY	WEDNESDAY	THURSDAY	FRIDAY	SATURDAY	SUNDAY
MEAL 1	Lettuce Cups	Stuffed Avocado Salad	Alkaline Electric Flatbread	Stuffed Avocado Salad	Spelt Strawberry Waffles	Alkaline Electric Flatbread	Arugula Salad
MEAL 2	Stuffed Bell Pepper	Classic Hummus	Stir-Fried Watercress	Spinach Bowl	Spinach Bowl	Vegan Apple Turnovers	Bone Broth
MEAL 3	Bone Broth	Home-Style Okra	Sesame Turnip Greens	Walnut Breakfast	Caramalized Strawberry ice-cream	Classic Hummus	Walnut Breakfast

WEEK 85	MONDAY	TUESDAY	WEDNESDAY	THURSDAY	FRIDAY	SATURDAY	SUNDAY
MEAL 1	Alkaline Veggie Fajitas	Alkaline Electric Tacos	Squash Falafels	Alkaline Electric Tacos	Stuffed Avocado Salad	Blueberries Muffins	Spelt grain salad
MEAL 2	Butternut Soup	Classic Hummus	Home-Style Okra	Bone Broth	Stuffed Bell Pepper	Stir-Fried Watercress	Kale Pesto
MEAL 3	Lettuce Cups	Mac & Cheese	Papaya Breakfast Shake	Creamy Kamut Pasta	Creamy Kamut Pasta	Papaya Breakfast Shake	Lettuce Cups

WEEK 86	MONDAY	TUESDAY	WEDNESDAY	THURSDAY	FRIDAY	SATURDAY	SUNDAY
MEAL 1	Curry Broccoli Salad	Fruity Yogurt	Arugula Salad	Alkaline Electric Flatbread	Spelt grain salad	Stuffed Avocado Salad	Lettuce Cups
MEAL 2	Bone Broth	Kale Pesto	Caramalized Strawberry ice-cream	Bone Broth	Home-Style Okra	Walnut Breakfast	Kale Pesto
MEAL 3	Rose Petals Honey	Canned Boneless Chicken	Rose Petals Honey	Canned Boneless Chicken	Mac & Cheese	Mac & Cheese	Mac & Cheese

WEEK 87	MONDAY	TUESDAY	WEDNESDAY	THURSDAY	FRIDAY	SATURDAY	SUNDAY
MEAL 1	Vegetable Patties	Spelt Strawberry Waffles	Curry Broccoli Salad	Blueberries Muffins	Spelt Pancakes	Stuffed Avocado Salad	Blueberries Muffins
MEAL 2	Caramalized Strawberry ice-cream	Vegan Apple Turnovers	Bone Broth	Spicy Soup	Classic Hummus	Bone Broth	The Greatest Greens
MEAL 3	Breakfast Skillet	Mexican-Style Quinoa	Mexican-Style Quinoa	Papaya Breakfast Shake	Veggie Omelette	Creamy Veggie Pasta	Mediterranean Kamut

WEEK 88	MONDAY	TUESDAY	WEDNESDAY	THURSDAY	FRIDAY	SATURDAY	SUNDAY
MEAL 1	Squash Falafels	Blueberries Muffins	Vegetable Patties	Curry Broccoli Salad	Fruity Yogurt	Fruity Yogurt	Stuffed Avocado Salad
MEAL 2	Roasted Okra	Fruit Skewers	Fruit Skewers	Spicy Soup	Butternut Soup	Fruit Skewers	Roasted Okra
MEAL 3	Mexican-Style Quinoa	Veggie Omelette	Strawberry ice-cream	Canned Boneless Chicken	Mexican-Style Quinoa	Rose Petals Honey	Rose Petals Honey

WEEK 89	MONDAY	TUESDAY	WEDNESDAY	THURSDAY	FRIDAY	SATURDAY	SUNDAY
MEAL 1	Spelt grain salad	Strawberry Ice Cream	Stuffed Avocado Salad	Spelt grain salad	Cucumber Dill Salad	Alkaline Electric Flatbread	Strawberry Ice Cream
MEAL 2	Vegan Apple Turnovers	Kale Pesto	Sesame Turnip Greens	Vegan Apple Turnovers	Home-Style Okra	Vegan Apple Turnovers	Sesame Turnip Greens
MEAL 3	Corn Relish	Lettuce Cups	Strawberry ice-cream	Mexican-Style Quinoa	Walnut Pesto Pasta	Mediterranean Kamut	Mac & Cheese

WEEK 90	MONDAY	TUESDAY	WEDNESDAY	THURSDAY	FRIDAY	SATURDAY	SUNDAY
MEAL 1	Blueberries Muffins	Stuffed Avocado Salad	Fruity Yogurt	Squash Falafels	Arugula Salad	Alkaline Electric Flatbread	Arugula Salad
MEAL 2	Caramalized Strawberry ice-cream	The Greatest Greens	Classic Hummus	Kale Pesto	Vegetable Mushroom Sauce	Roasted Okra	Butternut Soup
MEAL 3	Corn Relish	Mexican-Style Quinoa	Strawberry ice-cream	Electric Meatballs	Lettuce Cups	Mexican-Style Quinoa	Mexican-Style Quinoa

WEEK 91	MONDAY	TUESDAY	WEDNESDAY	THURSDAY	FRIDAY	SATURDAY	SUNDAY
MEAL 1	Spelt Strawberry Waffles	Savory Jumbo Pancakes	Banana Pancakes	Banana Pancakes	Spelt Strawberry Waffles	Spelt Pancakes	Blueberries Muffins
MEAL 2	Spicy Soup	Classic Hummus	Alkaline Zucchini Coleslaw	Home-Style Okra	Bone Broth	Wild Rice Stuffed Peppers	Butternut Soup
MEAL 3	Mac & Cheese	Alkaline Potato Salad	Corn Relish	Strawberry ice-cream	Chickpea Burger	Walnut Pesto Pasta	Alkaline Potato Salad

WEEK 92	MONDAY	TUESDAY	WEDNESDAY	THURSDAY	FRIDAY	SATURDAY	SUNDAY
MEAL 1	Stuffed Avocado Salad	Arugula Salad	Squash Falafels	Savory Jumbo Pancakes	Squash Falafels	Alkaline Electric Flatbread	Cinnamon Peach Jam
MEAL 2	Walnut Breakfast	Stir-Fried Watercress	Vegan Apple Turnovers	Stir-Fried Watercress	Fruit Skewers	Spinach Bowl	Butternut Soup
MEAL 3	Canned Boneless Chicken	Canned Boneless Chicken	Strawberry ice-cream	Corn Relish	Chickpea and Mushroom	Walnut Pesto Pasta	Pepper Relish

WEEK 93	MONDAY	TUESDAY	WEDNESDAY	THURSDAY	FRIDAY	SATURDAY	SUNDAY
MEAL 1	Spelt Strawberry Waffles	Spelt grain salad	Lettuce Cups	Cinnamon Peach Jam	Alkaline Electric Flatbread	Spelt Pancakes	Blueberries Muffins
MEAL 2	Spicy Soup	Alkaline Zucchini Coleslaw	Roasted Okra	Butternut Soup	Stuffed Bell Pepper	Caramalized Strawberry ice-cream	Bone Broth
MEAL 3	Mediterranean Kamut	Veggie Omelette	Chickpea and Mushroom	Mediterranean Kamut	Mac & Cheese	Mac & Cheese	Chickpea Burger

WEEK 94	MONDAY	TUESDAY	WEDNESDAY	THURSDAY	FRIDAY	SATURDAY	SUNDAY
MEAL 1	Alkaline Electric Flatbread	Fruity Yogurt	Savory Jumbo Pancakes	Vegetable Patties	Alkaline Electric Flatbread	Alkaline Veggie Fajitas	Curry Broccoli Salad
MEAL 2	Alkaline Zucchini Coleslaw	Stuffed Bell Pepper	Home-Style Okra	Caramalized Strawberry ice-cream	Zucchini Fritters	Vegan Apple Turnovers	Bone Broth
MEAL 3	Corn Relish	Canned Boneless Chicken	Canned Boneless Chicken	Garbanzo Burger	Garbanzo Burger	Mac & Cheese	Creamy Kamut Pasta

WEEK 95	MONDAY	TUESDAY	WEDNESDAY	THURSDAY	FRIDAY	SATURDAY	SUNDAY
MEAL 1	Spelt grain salad	Alkaline Electric Tacos	Savory Jumbo Pancakes	Alkaline Veggie Fajitas	Cinnamon Peach Jam	Alkaline Electric Tacos	Blueberries Muffins
MEAL 2	Vegan Apple Turnovers	Caramalized Strawberry ice-cream	Bone Broth	Spinach Bowl	Spinach Bowl	Vegetable Mushroom Sauce	Vegan Apple Turnovers
MEAL 3	Papaya Breakfast Shake	Creamy Veggie Pasta	Breakfast Skillet	Lettuce Cups	Strawberry ice-cream	Mac & Cheese	Mexican-Style Quinoa

WEEK 96	MONDAY	TUESDAY	WEDNESDAY	THURSDAY	FRIDAY	SATURDAY	SUNDAY
MEAL 1	Banana Pancakes	Spelt grain salad	Fruity Yogurt	Alkaline Veggie Fajitas	Spelt grain salad	Banana Pancakes	Alkaline Veggie Fajitas
MEAL 2	Wild Rice Stuffed Peppers	Spinach Bowl	Home-Style Okra	Spicy Soup	Bone Broth	Butternut Soup	Vegan Apple Turnovers
MEAL 3	Corn Relish	Creamy Kamut Pasta	Mediterranean Kamut	Mac & Cheese	Strawberry ice-cream	Pepper Relish	Walnut Pesto Pasta

WEEK 97	MONDAY	TUESDAY	WEDNESDAY	THURSDAY	FRIDAY	SATURDAY	SUNDAY
MEAL 1	Cucumber Dill Salad	Alkaline Electric Flatbread	Savory Jumbo Pancakes	Stuffed Avocado Salad	Banana Pancakes	Strawberry Ice Cream	Arugula Salad
MEAL 2	Roasted Okra	Spinach Bowl	Home-Style Okra	Wild Rice Stuffed Peppers	Zucchini Fritters	Home-Style Okra	Classic Hummus
MEAL 3	Pepper Relish	Mexican-Style Quinoa	Breakfast Skillet	Creamy Veggie Pasta	Chickpea Burger	Walnut Pesto Pasta	Veggie Omelette

WEEK 98	MONDAY	TUESDAY	WEDNESDAY	THURSDAY	FRIDAY	SATURDAY	SUNDAY
MEAL 1	Spelt Pancakes	Squash Falafels	Spelt grain salad	Spelt grain salad	Banana Pancakes	Cucumber Dill Salad	Lettuce Cups
MEAL 2	Butternut Soup	The Greatest Greens	Spicy Soup	Sesame Turnip Greens	Bone Broth	Classic Hummus	Sesame Turnip Greens
MEAL 3	Veggie Omelette	Mac & Cheese	Mexican-Style Quinoa	Corn Relish	Electric Meatballs	Strawberry ice-cream	Rose Petals Honey

WEEK 99	MONDAY	TUESDAY	WEDNESDAY	THURSDAY	FRIDAY	SATURDAY	SUNDAY
MEAL 1	Fruity Yogurt	Stuffed Avocado Salad	Arugula Salad	Vegetable Patties	Lettuce Cups	Strawberry Ice Cream	Lettuce Cups
MEAL 2	Walnut Breakfast	Roasted Okra	Walnut Breakfast	Classic Hummus	Vegan Apple Turnovers	Alkaline Zucchini Coleslaw	Spinach Bowl
MEAL 3	Breakfast Skillet	Electric Meatballs	Rose Petals Honey	Strawberry ice-cream	Mediterranean Kamut	Creamy Veggie Pasta	Mac & Cheese

WEEK 100	MONDAY	TUESDAY	WEDNESDAY	THURSDAY	FRIDAY	SATURDAY	SUNDAY
MEAL 1	Cinnamon Peach Jam	Cinnamon Peach Jam	Vegetable Patties	Fruity Yogurt	Cucumber Dill Salad	Squash Falafels	Alkaline Electric Flatbread
MEAL 2	Alkaline Zucchini Coleslaw	Roasted Okra	Kale Pesto	Vegetable Mushroom Sauce	Home-Style Okra	Alkaline Zucchini Coleslaw	Bone Broth
MEAL 3	Garbanzo Burger	Walnut Pesto Pasta	Pepper Relish	Pepper Relish	Papaya Breakfast Shake	Alkaline Potato Salad	Chickpea and Mushroom

WEEK 101	MONDAY	TUESDAY	WEDNESDAY	THURSDAY	FRIDAY	SATURDAY	SUNDAY
MEAL 1	Savory Jumbo Pancakes	Curry Broccoli Salad	Savory Jumbo Pancakes	Alkaline Veggie Fajitas	Herbed Mushroom Stew	Blueberries Muffins	Blueberries Muffins
MEAL 2	Bone Broth	Kale Pesto	Walnut Breakfast	Vegetable Mushroom Sauce	Vegan Apple Turnovers	Bone Broth	The Greatest Greens
MEAL 3	Breakfast Skillet	Veggie Omelette	Alkaline Potato Salad	Walnut Pesto Pasta	Mexican-Style Quinoa	Creamy Kamut Pasta	Chickpea Burger

WEEK 102	MONDAY	TUESDAY	WEDNESDAY	THURSDAY	FRIDAY	SATURDAY	SUNDAY
MEAL 1	Cinnamon Peach Jam	Cinnamon Peach Jam	Spelt Pancakes	Spelt Strawberry Waffles	Curry Broccoli Salad	Curry Broccoli Salad	Stuffed Avocado Salad
MEAL 2	Home-Style Okra	Caramalized Strawberry ice-cream	Stir-Fried Watercress	Sesame Turnip Greens	Spicy Soup	Roasted Okra	Sesame Turnip Greens
MEAL 3	Canned Boneless Chicken	Veggie Omelette	Papaya Breakfast Shake	Papaya Breakfast Shake	Creamy Kamut Pasta	Creamy Kamut Pasta	Veggie Omelette

WEEK 103	MONDAY	TUESDAY	WEDNESDAY	THURSDAY	FRIDAY	SATURDAY	SUNDAY
MEAL 1	Strawberry Ice Cream	Banana Pancakes	Alkaline Veggie Fajitas	Fruity Yogurt	Vegetable Patties	Spelt Pancakes	Spelt Pancakes
MEAL 2	Fruit Skewers	Vegetable Mushroom Sauce	Butternut Soup	Alkaline Zucchini Coleslaw	Sesame Turnip Greens	Roasted Okra	Classic Hummus
MEAL 3	Veggie Omelette	Pepper Relish	Chickpea and Mushroom	Mexican-Style Quinoa	Veggie Omelette	Garbanzo Burger	Papaya Breakfast Shake

WEEK 104	MONDAY	TUESDAY	WEDNESDAY	THURSDAY	FRIDAY	SATURDAY	SUNDAY
MEAL 1	Banana Pancakes	Herbed Mushroom Stew	Lettuce Cups	Alkaline Veggie Fajitas	Alkaline Veggie Fajitas	Spelt Strawberry Waffles	Alkaline Electric Flatbread
MEAL 2	Bone Broth	Bone Broth	Walnut Breakfast	Alkaline Zucchini Coleslaw	Alkaline Zucchini Coleslaw	Stuffed Bell Pepper	Wild Rice Stuffed Peppers
MEAL 3	Strawberry ice-cream	Veggie Omelette	Alkaline Potato Salad	Papaya Breakfast Shake	Creamy Veggie Pasta	Canned Boneless Chicken	Lettuce Cups

WEEK 105	MONDAY	TUESDAY	WEDNESDAY	THURSDAY	FRIDAY	SATURDAY	SUNDAY
MEAL 1	Cucumber Dill Salad	Savory Jumbo Pancakes	Cucumber Dill Salad	Spelt grain salad	Vegetable Patties	Banana Pancakes	Herbed Mushroom Stew
MEAL 2	Stuffed Bell Pepper	Bone Broth	Walnut Breakfast	Bone Broth	Vegan Apple Turnovers	Spicy Soup	Bone Broth
MEAL 3	Alkaline Potato Salad	Papaya Breakfast Shake	Rose Petals Honey	Veggie Omelette	Electric Meatballs	Creamy Veggie Pasta	Chickpea Burger

WEEK 106	MONDAY	TUESDAY	WEDNESDAY	THURSDAY	FRIDAY	SATURDAY	SUNDAY
MEAL 1	Vegetable Patties	Stuffed Avocado Salad	Stuffed Avocado Salad	Strawberry Ice Cream	Spelt grain salad	Alkaline Electric Tacos	Vegetable Patties
MEAL 2	Wild Rice Stuffed Peppers	The Greatest Greens	Vegan Apple Turnovers	Caramalized Strawberry ice-cream	Spinach Bowl	Caramalized Strawberry ice-cream	Roasted Okra
MEAL 3	Mac & Cheese	Corn Relish	Electric Meatballs	Chickpea and Mushroom	Strawberry ice-cream	Creamy Kamut Pasta	Corn Relish

WEEK 107	MONDAY	TUESDAY	WEDNESDAY	THURSDAY	FRIDAY	SATURDAY	SUNDAY
MEAL 1	Alkaline Electric Tacos	Alkaline Electric Tacos	Spelt Strawberry Waffles	Cinnamon Peach Jam	Spelt grain salad	Cinnamon Peach Jam	Spelt Pancakes
MEAL 2	Vegetable Mushroom Sauce	Spicy Soup	Spinach Bowl	Vegetable Mushroom Sauce	Stir-Fried Watercress	Roasted Okra	Alkaline Zucchini Coleslaw
MEAL 3	Corn Relish	Creamy Kamut Pasta	Strawberry ice-cream	Rose Petals Honey	Lettuce Cups	Garbanzo Burger	Strawberry ice-cream

WEEK 108	MONDAY	TUESDAY	WEDNESDAY	THURSDAY	FRIDAY	SATURDAY	SUNDAY
MEAL 1	Cucumber Dill Salad	Fruity Yogurt	Spelt Pancakes	Spelt Pancakes	Blueberries Muffins	Alkaline Veggie Fajitas	Strawberry Ice Cream
MEAL 2	The Greatest Greens	Bone Broth	Home-Style Okra	Fruit Skewers	Vegetable Mushroom Sauce	Kale Pesto	Classic Hummus
MEAL 3	Electric Meatballs	Chickpea and Mushroom	Veggie Omelette	Walnut Pesto Pasta	Creamy Veggie Pasta	Electric Meatballs	Garbanzo Burger

WEEK 109	MONDAY	TUESDAY	WEDNESDAY	THURSDAY	FRIDAY	SATURDAY	SUNDAY
MEAL 1	Curry Broccoli Salad	Strawberry Ice Cream	Herbed Mushroom Stew	Spelt Pancakes	Savory Jumbo Pancakes	Curry Broccoli Salad	Lettuce Cups
MEAL 2	Sesame Turnip Greens	Spinach Bowl	Alkaline Zucchini Coleslaw	Butternut Soup	Walnut Breakfast	Caramalized Strawberry ice-cream	Walnut Breakfast
MEAL 3	Mac & Cheese	Creamy Kamut Pasta	Pepper Relish	Papaya Breakfast Shake	Creamy Kamut Pasta	Mac & Cheese	Mexican-Style Quinoa

WEEK 110	MONDAY	TUESDAY	WEDNESDAY	THURSDAY	FRIDAY	SATURDAY	SUNDAY
MEAL 1	Cinnamon Peach Jam	Arugula Salad	Spelt Pancakes	Spelt grain salad	Stuffed Avocado Salad	Curry Broccoli Salad	Stuffed Avocado Salad
MEAL 2	Alkaline Zucchini Coleslaw	Walnut Breakfast	Spicy Soup	The Greatest Greens	Alkaline Zucchini Coleslaw	Stuffed Bell Pepper	Wild Rice Stuffed Peppers
MEAL 3	Chickpea Burger	Breakfast Skillet	Chickpea and Mushroom	Electric Meatballs	Breakfast Skillet	Breakfast Skillet	Pepper Relish

WEEK 111	MONDAY	TUESDAY	WEDNESDAY	THURSDAY	FRIDAY	SATURDAY	SUNDAY
MEAL 1	Arugula Salad	Spelt Pancakes	Lettuce Cups	Spelt grain salad	Alkaline Electric Tacos	Blueberries Muffins	Squash Falafels
MEAL 2	Walnut Breakfast	Home-Style Okra	The Greatest Greens	Butternut Soup	Spinach Bowl	Stir-Fried Watercress	Spicy Soup
MEAL 3	Mexican-Style Quinoa	Electric Meatballs	Pepper Relish	Chickpea Burger	Veggie Omelette	Mexican-Style Quinoa	Strawberry ice-cream

WEEK 112	MONDAY	TUESDAY	WEDNESDAY	THURSDAY	FRIDAY	SATURDAY	SUNDAY
MEAL 1	Cucumber Dill Salad	Blueberries Muffins	Strawberry Ice Cream	Lettuce Cups	Blueberries Muffins	Banana Pancakes	Cucumber Dill Salad
MEAL 2	Stuffed Bell Pepper	Spicy Soup	The Greatest Greens	Bone Broth	Wild Rice Stuffed Peppers	Stuffed Bell Pepper	Vegetable Mushroom Sauce
MEAL 3	Veggie Omelette	Lettuce Cups	Pepper Relish	Mediterranean Kamut	Papaya Breakfast Shake	Alkaline Potato Salad	Canned Boneless Chicken

WEEK 113	MONDAY	TUESDAY	WEDNESDAY	THURSDAY	FRIDAY	SATURDAY	SUNDAY
MEAL 1	Spelt Pancakes	Herbed Mushroom Stew	Arugula Salad	Cucumber Dill Salad	Fruity Yogurt	Fruity Yogurt	Alkaline Electric Flatbread
MEAL 2	Stuffed Bell Pepper	Spinach Bowl	Bone Broth	Spicy Soup	Home-Style Okra	Bone Broth	Wild Rice Stuffed Peppers
MEAL 3	Lettuce Cups	Papaya Breakfast Shake	Mexican-Style Quinoa	Chickpea Burger	Breakfast Skillet	Veggie Omelette	Mexican-Style Quinoa

WEEK 114	MONDAY	TUESDAY	WEDNESDAY	THURSDAY	FRIDAY	SATURDAY	SUNDAY
MEAL 1	Fruity Yogurt	Banana Pancakes	Blueberries Muffins	Spelt Strawberry Waffles	Savory Jumbo Pancakes	Alkaline Electric Tacos	Savory Jumbo Pancakes
MEAL 2	The Greatest Greens	Stuffed Bell Pepper	Walnut Breakfast	Stir-Fried Watercress	Butternut Soup	Spinach Bowl	Wild Rice Stuffed Peppers
MEAL 3	Strawberry ice-cream	Veggie Omelette	Papaya Breakfast Shake	Alkaline Potato Salad	Alkaline Potato Salad	Alkaline Potato Salad	Chickpea and Mushroom

WEEK 115	MONDAY	TUESDAY	WEDNESDAY	THURSDAY	FRIDAY	SATURDAY	SUNDAY
MEAL 1	Stuffed Avocado Salad	Arugula Salad	Alkaline Electric Flatbread	Spelt grain salad	Strawberry Ice Cream	Herbed Mushroom Stew	Stuffed Avocado Salad
MEAL 2	Wild Rice Stuffed Peppers	Caramalized Strawberry ice-cream	Roasted Okra	Roasted Okra	Kale Pesto	Spinach Bowl	Walnut Breakfast
MEAL 3	Chickpea and Mushroom	Creamy Veggie Pasta	Creamy Kamut Pasta	Papaya Breakfast Shake	Electric Meatballs	Veggie Omelette	Creamy Kamut Pasta

WEEK 116	MONDAY	TUESDAY	WEDNESDAY	THURSDAY	FRIDAY	SATURDAY	SUNDAY
MEAL 1	Lettuce Cups	Banana Pancakes	Herbed Mushroom Stew	Vegetable Patties	Banana Pancakes	Curry Broccoli Salad	Cucumber Dill Salad
MEAL 2	Butternut Soup	Bone Broth	Walnut Breakfast	Alkaline Zucchini Coleslaw	Wild Rice Stuffed Peppers	Sesame Turnip Greens	Vegan Apple Turnovers
MEAL 3	Wild Rice Stuffed Peppers	Caramalized Strawberry ice-cream	Roasted Okra	Roasted Okra	Kale Pesto	Spinach Bowl	Walnut Breakfast

WEEK 117	MONDAY	TUESDAY	WEDNESDAY	THURSDAY	FRIDAY	SATURDAY	SUNDAY
MEAL 1	Alkaline Electric Tacos	Cucumber Dill Salad	Savory Jumbo Pancakes	Arugula Salad	Spelt grain salad	Strawberry Ice Cream	Arugula Salad
MEAL 2	Zucchini Fritters	The Greatest Greens	Spinach Bowl	Vegan Apple Turnovers	Vegan Apple Turnovers	Vegan Apple Turnovers	Home-Style Okra
MEAL 3	Lettuce Cups	Walnut Pesto Pasta	Rose Petals Honey	Chickpea and Mushroom	Breakfast Skillet	Walnut Pesto Pasta	Electric Meatballs

WEEK 118	MONDAY	TUESDAY	WEDNESDAY	THURSDAY	FRIDAY	SATURDAY	SUNDAY
MEAL 1	Cucumber Dill Salad	Cucumber Dill Salad	Herbed Mushroom Stew	Arugula Salad	Cinnamon Peach Jam	Spelt grain salad	Spelt grain salad
MEAL 2	Wild Rice Stuffed Peppers	Roasted Okra	Home-Style Okra	Home-Style Okra	Spicy Soup	Kale Pesto	Stuffed Bell Pepper
MEAL 3	Walnut Pesto Pasta	Canned Boneless Chicken	Electric Meatballs	Canned Boneless Chicken	Mexican-Style Quinoa	Electric Meatballs	Rose Petals Honey

WEEK 119	MONDAY	TUESDAY	WEDNESDAY	THURSDAY	FRIDAY	SATURDAY	SUNDAY
MEAL 1	Savory Jumbo Pancakes	Alkaline Veggie Fajitas	Stuffed Avocado Salad	Blueberries Muffins	Curry Broccoli Salad	Cinnamon Peach Jam	Savory Jumbo Pancakes
MEAL 2	Classic Hummus	Vegetable Mushroom Sauce	Home-Style Okra	Stuffed Bell Pepper	Stuffed Bell Pepper	Walnut Breakfast	The Greatest Greens
MEAL 3	Breakfast Skillet	Rose Petals Honey	Walnut Pesto Pasta	Mexican-Style Quinoa	Veggie Omelette	Strawberry ice-cream	Mediterranean Kamut

WEEK 120	MONDAY	TUESDAY	WEDNESDAY	THURSDAY	FRIDAY	SATURDAY	SUNDAY
MEAL 1	Alkaline Electric Tacos	Strawberry Ice Cream	Spelt Pancakes	Spelt Pancakes	Alkaline Electric Tacos	Strawberry Ice Cream	Savory Jumbo Pancakes
MEAL 2	Walnut Breakfast	Vegan Apple Turnovers	Wild Rice Stuffed Peppers	Wild Rice Stuffed Peppers	Caramalized Strawberry ice-cream	Zucchini Fritters	Sesame Turnip Greens
MEAL 3	Walnut Pesto Pasta	Electric Meatballs	Strawberry ice-cream	Mediterranean Kamut	Alkaline Potato Salad	Papaya Breakfast Shake	Mexican-Style Quinoa

WEEK 121	MONDAY	TUESDAY	WEDNESDAY	THURSDAY	FRIDAY	SATURDAY	SUNDAY
MEAL 1	Blueberries Muffins	Cinnamon Peach Jam	Blueberries Muffins	Stuffed Avocado Salad	Vegetable Patties	Alkaline Veggie Fajitas	Herbed Mushroom Stew
MEAL 2	Classic Hummus	Caramalized Strawberry ice-cream	Fruit Skewers	Wild Rice Stuffed Peppers	Butternut Soup	Walnut Breakfast	Walnut Breakfast
MEAL 3	Garbanzo Burger	Chickpea and Mushroom	Pepper Relish	Creamy Veggie Pasta	Chickpea Burger	Chickpea and Mushroom	Breakfast Skillet

WEEK 122	MONDAY	TUESDAY	WEDNESDAY	THURSDAY	FRIDAY	SATURDAY	SUNDAY
MEAL 1	Strawberry Ice Cream	Spelt grain salad	Lettuce Cups	Savory Jumbo Pancakes	Arugula Salad	Cinnamon Peach Jam	Squash Falafels
MEAL 2	Walnut Breakfast	Butternut Soup	The Greatest Greens	Zucchini Fritters	Roasted Okra	Butternut Soup	Stir-Fried Watercress
MEAL 3	Garbanzo Burger	Lettuce Cups	Strawberry ice-cream	Rose Petals Honey	Veggie Omelette	Walnut Pesto Pasta	Papaya Breakfast Shake

WEEK 123	MONDAY	TUESDAY	WEDNESDAY	THURSDAY	FRIDAY	SATURDAY	SUNDAY
MEAL 1	Banana Pancakes	Strawberry Ice Cream	Spelt grain salad	Cinnamon Peach Jam	Stuffed Avocado Salad	Strawberry Ice Cream	Arugula Salad
MEAL 2	Stir-Fried Watercress	Wild Rice Stuffed Peppers	Stir-Fried Watercress	Caramalized Strawberry ice-cream	Bone Broth	Vegan Apple Turnovers	Stuffed Bell Pepper
MEAL 3	Breakfast Skillet	Strawberry ice-cream	Rose Petals Honey	Walnut Pesto Pasta	Electric Meatballs	Chickpea and Mushroom	Chickpea and Mushroom

WEEK 124	MONDAY	TUESDAY	WEDNESDAY	THURSDAY	FRIDAY	SATURDAY	SUNDAY
MEAL 1	Savory Jumbo Pancakes	Savory Jumbo Pancakes	Savory Jumbo Pancakes	Lettuce Cups	Banana Pancakes	Vegetable Patties	Alkaline Veggie Fajitas
MEAL 2	The Greatest Greens	Classic Hummus	Walnut Breakfast	Bone Broth	Classic Hummus	Walnut Breakfast	Classic Hummus
MEAL 3	Papaya Breakfast Shake	Canned Boneless Chicken	Creamy Kamut Pasta	Papaya Breakfast Shake	Papaya Breakfast Shake	Strawberry ice-cream	Corn Relish

WEEK 125	MONDAY	TUESDAY	WEDNESDAY	THURSDAY	FRIDAY	SATURDAY	SUNDAY
MEAL 1	Arugula Salad	Spelt Strawberry Waffles	Spelt Strawberry Waffles	Herbed Mushroom Stew	Alkaline Electric Flatbread	Cinnamon Peach Jam	Cinnamon Peach Jam
MEAL 2	Classic Hummus	Fruit Skewers	Vegan Apple Turnovers	Classic Hummus	Stuffed Bell Pepper	Spinach Bowl	Zucchini Fritters
MEAL 3	Strawberry ice-cream	Mediterranean Kamut	Electric Meatballs	Chickpea Burger	Walnut Pesto Pasta	Walnut Pesto Pasta	Corn Relish

WEEK 126	MONDAY	TUESDAY	WEDNESDAY	THURSDAY	FRIDAY	SATURDAY	SUNDAY
MEAL 1	Banana Pancakes	Fruity Yogurt	Alkaline Electric Tacos	Strawberry Ice Cream	Alkaline Electric Flatbread	Spelt grain salad	Lettuce Cups
MEAL 2	Spinach Bowl	Alkaline Zucchini Coleslaw	Butternut Soup	Spinach Bowl	Spinach Bowl	Classic Hummus	Zucchini Fritters
MEAL 3	Pepper Relish	Corn Relish	Papaya Breakfast Shake	Electric Meatballs	Mac & Cheese	Veggie Omelette	Breakfast Skillet

WEEK 127	MONDAY	TUESDAY	WEDNESDAY	THURSDAY	FRIDAY	SATURDAY	SUNDAY
MEAL 1	Squash Falafels	Herbed Mushroom Stew	Strawberry Ice Cream	Cucumber Dill Salad	Fruity Yogurt	Spelt Strawberry Waffles	Stuffed Avocado Salad
MEAL 2	Vegan Apple Turnovers	Kale Pesto	Home-Style Okra	Vegetable Mushroom Sauce	Bone Broth	Butternut Soup	Alkaline Zucchini Coleslaw
MEAL 3	Lettuce Cups	Rose Petals Honey	Strawberry ice-cream	Electric Meatballs	Canned Boneless Chicken	Lettuce Cups	Canned Boneless Chicken

WEEK 128	MONDAY	TUESDAY	WEDNESDAY	THURSDAY	FRIDAY	SATURDAY	SUNDAY
MEAL 1	Vegetable Patties	Spelt Strawberry Waffles	Savory Jumbo Pancakes	Blueberries Muffins	Squash Falafels	Spelt Strawberry Waffles	Savory Jumbo Pancakes
MEAL 2	Stir-Fried Watercress	Classic Hummus	Vegan Apple Turnovers	Classic Hummus	Butternut Soup	Spicy Soup	Caramalized Strawberry ice-cream
MEAL 3	Strawberry ice-cream	Mac & Cheese	Strawberry ice-cream	Pepper Relish	Rose Petals Honey	Creamy Veggie Pasta	Chickpea and Mushroom

WEEK 129	MONDAY	TUESDAY	WEDNESDAY	THURSDAY	FRIDAY	SATURDAY	SUNDAY
MEAL 1	Lettuce Cups	Lettuce Cups	Alkaline Electric Tacos	Spelt Pancakes	Arugula Salad	Alkaline Electric Flatbread	Alkaline Electric Tacos
MEAL 2	Spinach Bowl	The Greatest Greens	Roasted Okra	Walnut Breakfast	Kale Pesto	Spicy Soup	Home-Style Okra
MEAL 3	Walnut Pesto Pasta	Canned Boneless Chicken	Garbanzo Burger	Mac & Cheese	Mac & Cheese	Rose Petals Honey	Corn Relish

WEEK 130	MONDAY	TUESDAY	WEDNESDAY	THURSDAY	FRIDAY	SATURDAY	SUNDAY
MEAL 1	Fruity Yogurt	Banana Pancakes	Blueberries Muffins	Alkaline Veggie Fajitas	Blueberries Muffins	Spelt Pancakes	Stuffed Avocado Salad
MEAL 2	Home-Style Okra	Butternut Soup	Bone Broth	Classic Hummus	Stir-Fried Watercress	Stir-Fried Watercress	Home-Style Okra
MEAL 3	Mac & Cheese	Creamy Veggie Pasta	Creamy Veggie Pasta	Mac & Cheese	Mac & Cheese	Creamy Veggie Pasta	Papaya Breakfast Shake

WEEK 131	MONDAY	TUESDAY	WEDNESDAY	THURSDAY	FRIDAY	SATURDAY	SUNDAY
MEAL 1	Blueberries Muffins	Vegetable Patties	Stuffed Avocado Salad	Blueberries Muffins	Alkaline Veggie Fajitas	Banana Pancakes	Strawberry Ice Cream
MEAL 2	Sesame Turnip Greens	Vegan Apple Turnovers	Spinach Bowl	Stir-Fried Watercress	Spinach Bowl	Wild Rice Stuffed Peppers	Caramalized Strawberry ice-cream
MEAL 3	Electric Meatballs	Mexican-Style Quinoa	Lettuce Cups	Corn Relish	Chickpea and Mushroom	Strawberry ice-cream	Mexican-Style Quinoa

WEEK 132	MONDAY	TUESDAY	WEDNESDAY	THURSDAY	FRIDAY	SATURDAY	SUNDAY
MEAL 1	Spelt Pancakes	Squash Falafels	Savory Jumbo Pancakes	Cinnamon Peach Jam	Strawberry Ice Cream	Herbed Mushroom Stew	Arugula Salad
MEAL 2	Stuffed Bell Pepper	Wild Rice Stuffed Peppers	Stir-Fried Watercress	Vegan Apple Turnovers	Bone Broth	Bone Broth	Zucchini Fritters
MEAL 3	Creamy Veggie Pasta	Alkaline Potato Salad	Strawberry ice-cream	Canned Boneless Chicken	Electric Meatballs	Garbanzo Burger	Mexican-Style Quinoa

WEEK 133	MONDAY	TUESDAY	WEDNESDAY	THURSDAY	FRIDAY	SATURDAY	SUNDAY
MEAL 1	Alkaline Electric Flatbread	Spelt grain salad	Stuffed Avocado Salad	Alkaline Veggie Fajitas	Cucumber Dill Salad	Spelt grain salad	Alkaline Veggie Fajitas
MEAL 2	The Greatest Greens	Sesame Turnip Greens	Fruit Skewers	Alkaline Zucchini Coleslaw	Bone Broth	Spinach Bowl	Stuffed Bell Pepper
MEAL 3	Creamy Kamut Pasta	Lettuce Cups	Breakfast Skillet	Garbanzo Burger	Walnut Pesto Pasta	Pepper Relish	Electric Meatballs

WEEK 134	MONDAY	TUESDAY	WEDNESDAY	THURSDAY	FRIDAY	SATURDAY	SUNDAY
MEAL 1	Arugula Salad	Savory Jumbo Pancakes	Curry Broccoli Salad	Alkaline Veggie Fajitas	Spelt grain salad	Strawberry Ice Cream	Stuffed Avocado Salad
MEAL 2	Spicy Soup	Kale Pesto	Vegetable Mushroom Sauce	Spicy Soup	Sesame Turnip Greens	Home-Style Okra	Stuffed Bell Pepper
MEAL 3	Chickpea and Mushroom	Creamy Kamut Pasta	Creamy Kamut Pasta	Garbanzo Burger	Electric Meatballs	Garbanzo Burger	Creamy Kamut Pasta

WEEK 135	MONDAY	TUESDAY	WEDNESDAY	THURSDAY	FRIDAY	SATURDAY	SUNDAY
MEAL 1	Vegetable Patties	Spelt Pancakes	Fruity Yogurt	Spelt Strawberry Waffles	Curry Broccoli Salad	Fruity Yogurt	Blueberries Muffins
MEAL 2	Bone Broth	Kale Pesto	Alkaline Zucchini Coleslaw	Home-Style Okra	Stir-Fried Watercress	The Greatest Greens	Roasted Okra
MEAL 3	Creamy Veggie Pasta	Alkaline Potato Salad	Breakfast Skillet	Chickpea and Mushroom	Chickpea and Mushroom	Corn Relish	Lettuce Cups

WEEK 136	MONDAY	TUESDAY	WEDNESDAY	THURSDAY	FRIDAY	SATURDAY	SUNDAY
MEAL 1	Squash Falafels	Alkaline Electric Tacos	Alkaline Electric Tacos	Strawberry Ice Cream	Curry Broccoli Salad	Banana Pancakes	Curry Broccoli Salad
MEAL 2	Sesame Turnip Greens	Wild Rice Stuffed Peppers	Stir-Fried Watercress	Alkaline Zucchini Coleslaw	Stir-Fried Watercress	Home-Style Okra	Walnut Breakfast
MEAL 3	Veggie Omelette	Veggie Omelette	Walnut Pesto Pasta	Breakfast Skillet	Alkaline Potato Salad	Mediterranean Kamut	Lettuce Cups

WEEK 137	MONDAY	TUESDAY	WEDNESDAY	THURSDAY	FRIDAY	SATURDAY	SUNDAY
MEAL 1	Spelt Strawberry Waffles	Cinnamon Peach Jam	Alkaline Electric Tacos	Curry Broccoli Salad	Alkaline Veggie Fajitas	Blueberries Muffins	Lettuce Cups
MEAL 2	Classic Hummus	The Greatest Greens	Zucchini Fritters	Walnut Breakfast	Roasted Okra	Roasted Okra	Stuffed Bell Pepper
MEAL 3	Creamy Veggie Pasta	Mexican-Style Quinoa	Chickpea and Mushroom	Chickpea Burger	Corn Relish	Papaya Breakfast Shake	Creamy Veggie Pasta

WEEK 138	MONDAY	TUESDAY	WEDNESDAY	THURSDAY	FRIDAY	SATURDAY	SUNDAY
MEAL 1	Banana Pancakes	Squash Falafels	Arugula Salad	Lettuce Cups	Alkaline Veggie Fajitas	Savory Jumbo Pancakes	Strawberry Ice Cream
MEAL 2	Stir-Fried Watercress	Fruit Skewers	Stir-Fried Watercress	Zucchini Fritters	Kale Pesto	Spinach Bowl	Vegan Apple Turnovers
MEAL 3	Electric Meatballs	Mexican-Style Quinoa	Creamy Kamut Pasta	Papaya Breakfast Shake	Mexican-Style Quinoa	Electric Meatballs	Creamy Veggie Pasta

WEEK 139	MONDAY	TUESDAY	WEDNESDAY	THURSDAY	FRIDAY	SATURDAY	SUNDAY
MEAL 1	Stuffed Avocado Salad	Strawberry Ice Cream	Squash Falafels	Curry Broccoli Salad	Cucumber Dill Salad	Lettuce Cups	Alkaline Electric Tacos
MEAL 2	Kale Pesto	Spicy Soup	Vegetable Mushroom Sauce	The Greatest Greens	Caramalized Strawberry ice-cream	Vegan Apple Turnovers	Vegetable Mushroom Sauce
MEAL 3	Creamy Veggie Pasta	Chickpea Burger	Veggie Omelette	Papaya Breakfast Shake	Walnut Pesto Pasta	Rose Petals Honey	Garbanzo Burger

WEEK 140	MONDAY	TUESDAY	WEDNESDAY	THURSDAY	FRIDAY	SATURDAY	SUNDAY
MEAL 1	Stuffed Avocado Salad	Squash Falafels	Spelt Strawberry Waffles	Fruity Yogurt	Stuffed Avocado Salad	Curry Broccoli Salad	Lettuce Cups
MEAL 2	Classic Hummus	Stuffed Bell Pepper	The Greatest Greens	Spinach Bowl	Spinach Bowl	Fruit Skewers	Butternut Soup
MEAL 3	Rose Petals Honey	Breakfast Skillet	Chickpea Burger	Veggie Omelette	Pepper Relish	Papaya Breakfast Shake	Garbanzo Burger

WEEK 141	MONDAY	TUESDAY	WEDNESDAY	THURSDAY	FRIDAY	SATURDAY	SUNDAY
MEAL 1	Vegetable Patties	Lettuce Cups	Curry Broccoli Salad	Banana Pancakes	Strawberry Ice Cream	Vegetable Patties	Banana Pancakes
MEAL 2	Vegetable Mushroom Sauce	Caramalized Strawberry ice-cream	Wild Rice Stuffed Peppers	Walnut Breakfast	Alkaline Zucchini Coleslaw	Kale Pesto	The Greatest Greens
MEAL 3	Garbanzo Burger	Canned Boneless Chicken	Corn Relish	Papaya Breakfast Shake	Pepper Relish	Creamy Kamut Pasta	Chickpea and Mushroom

WEEK 142	MONDAY	TUESDAY	WEDNESDAY	THURSDAY	FRIDAY	SATURDAY	SUNDAY
MEAL 1	Vegetable Patties	Cucumber Dill Salad	Spelt Strawberry Waffles	Stuffed Avocado Salad	Spelt grain salad	Arugula Salad	Blueberries Muffins
MEAL 2	Wild Rice Stuffed Peppers	Zucchini Fritters	The Greatest Greens	Fruit Skewers	Home-Style Okra	Home-Style Okra	Sesame Turnip Greens
MEAL 3	Creamy Kamut Pasta	Corn Relish	Creamy Kamut Pasta	Creamy Kamut Pasta	Breakfast Skillet	Veggie Omelette	Veggie Omelette

WEEK 143	MONDAY	TUESDAY	WEDNESDAY	THURSDAY	FRIDAY	SATURDAY	SUNDAY
MEAL 1	Alkaline Veggie Fajitas	Blueberries Muffins	Squash Falafels	Lettuce Cups	Cucumber Dill Salad	Cucumber Dill Salad	Blueberries Muffins
MEAL 2	Caramalized Strawberry ice-cream	Classic Hummus	Caramalized Strawberry ice-cream	Classic Hummus	Bone Broth	Butternut Soup	Stir-Fried Watercress
MEAL 3	Rose Petals Honey	Walnut Pesto Pasta	Breakfast Skillet	Rose Petals Honey	Corn Relish	Mediterranean Kamut	Rose Petals Honey

Made in the USA
Coppell, TX
27 October 2021